T

TWICE UPON A TIME

Recent Titles in the
Children's and Young Adult Literature Reference Series
Catherine Barr, Series Editor

Books Kids Will Sit Still For 3: A Read-Aloud Guide
Judy Freeman

Classic Teenplots: A Booktalk Guide to Use with Readers Ages 12–18
John T. Gillespie and Corinne J. Naden

Best Books for Middle School and Junior High Readers: Grades 6–9.
Supplement to the First Edition
John T. Gillespie and Catherine Barr

Best Books for High School Readers: Grades 9–12. Supplement to the First Edition
John T. Gillespie and Catherine Barr

War and Peace: A Guide to Literature and New Media, Grades 4–8
Virginia A. Walter

Across Cultures: A Guide to Multicultural Literature for Children
Kathy East and Rebecca L. Thomas

Best Books for Children, Supplement to the 8th Edition: Preschool through Grade 6
Catherine Barr and John T. Gillespie

Best Books for Boys: A Resource for Educators
Matthew D. Zbaracki

Beyond Picture Books: Subject Access to Best Books for Beginning Readers
Barbara Barstow, Judith Riggle, and Leslie Molnar

A to Zoo: Subject Access to Children's Picture Books. Supplement to the 7th Edition
Carolyn W. Lima and Rebecca L. Thomas

Gentle Reads: Great Books to Warm Hearts and Lift Spirits, Grades 5–9
Deanna J. McDaniel

Best New Media, K–12 : A Guide to Movies, Subscription Web Sites, and Educational
Software and Games
Catherine Barr

TWICE UPON A TIME

A Guide to Fractured, Altered, and Retold Folk and Fairy Tales

CATHARINE BOMHOLD AND TERRI E. ELDER

Children's and Young Adult Literature Reference
Catherine Barr, Series Editor

LIBRARIES
U N L I M I T E D
A Member of the Greenwood Publishing Group

Westport, Connecticut • London

Library of Congress Cataloging-in-Publication Data

Bomhold, Catharine, 1966-
  Twice upon a time / a guide to fractured, altered, and retold folk and fairy tales / Catharine
Bomhold and Terri E. Elder.
      p. cm. — (Children's and young adult literature reference)
  Includes bibliographical references and indexes.
  ISBN 978-1-59158-390-5 (alk. paper)
  1. Children's literature—Bibliography. 2. Children—Books and reading. 3. Folk literature—
Bibliography. 4. Fairy tales—Bibliography. I. Elder, Terri E. II. Title.
  Z1037.B714 2008
  011.62—dc22   2008034683

British Library Cataloguing in Publication Data is available.

Library of Congress Catalog Card Number: 2008034683
ISBN: 978-1-59158-390-5

First published in 2008

Libraries Unlimited, 88 Post Road West, Westport, CT 06881
A Member of the Greenwood Publishing Group, Inc.
www.lu.com

Printed in the United States of America

The paper used in this book complies with the
Permanent Paper Standard issued by the National
Information Standards Organization (Z39.48–1984).

10 9 8 7 6 5 4 3 2 1

CONTENTS

PREFACE

MOST CASUAL READERS HAVE A CONCEPT OF WHAT FAIRY tales are. Scholars categorize such stories—defined as "magical tales"— as one of four subtypes of folktales. Folktales—commonplace narratives employing ordinary protagonists—also include jokes, fables, and novellas, and belong to the literary genre of folk narrative, which also includes myths and legends.

But for the average reader, this definition may be too restrictive. The folksonomy of fairy tales includes a wide variety of stories that may or may not include fairies or magic and that might be better defined as "wonder tales." Most are known as children's stories, regardless of the reader's age. They include tales from the oral tradition that have been collected and recorded by recognized names such as Grimm, Perrault, Jacobs, Andersen, and Aesop, and they have existed in popular memory for centuries. This bibliography is not restricted by academic definitions, but includes folk stories, fables, and fairy tales well known to the general public.

Originally meant to gather only the humorous and sometimes silly revisions of the most common tales, the variety of retellings demanded that we expand our criteria for inclusion in this work. After surveying OCLC holdings, it was found that retellings can fall into four general and sometimes overlapping categories. The first two types, the unconventional revisions and the slightly modified, include the titles that were the original intent of this study. The unconventional stories include many popular favorites such as *Cinder-Edna* (Jackson and O'Malley), *The True Story of the Three Little Pigs* (Scieszka and Smith), and *The Three Pigs* (Wiesner). These titles are hilarious and brazen rewrites of traditional texts meant to challenge young readers by presenting them in the theater of the absurd. The second type—tales that are considered modified—relate the story much as we know it but change details or plotlines enough to make the story overtly different. Common changes include the incorporation of dialect, contemporary settings, and unusual or revised endings. Jack and the Beanstalk and Red

Riding Hood have many versions that accentuate the main character's flaws (breaking and entering; stealing) and provide 21st-century-appropriate consequences. Both of these types of fractured tales, the unconventional and the modified, are also marked by a large number of titles that use gender role reversal as a catalyst for revision.

Two other story types were a byproduct of the original research. First of these are familiar tales that are set in cultures foreign to Anglo Americans. Many are story types as described in the Aarne-Thompson classification system. They coincide with western story types but the stories themselves are native to other cultures. Tam and Cam is an example—a Vietnamese version of Aarne-Thompson type 510 also known in the West as Cinderella. And the second group is western tales that have been revised for American audiences by setting them in a different country or culture. Eric Kimmel's *Cactus Soup* (2004) is a version of Stone Soup set in Mexico, and Sheila Hébert-Collins has authored several volumes of popular tales with Cajun themes. The purpose of this type of revision can be both entertainment and education. Tales are often reset in another country or culture in order to make the plot more accessible to a diverse population of children, or to provide all children with some knowledge of other cultures.

This bibliography collects and annotates popular folk and fairy tale titles that may not be included in the wide variety of bibliographies of children's books available because they have been altered in some manner from the Anglo American version. From the global and indispensable *A to Zoo: A Subject Guide to Picture Books* to age-specific compilations such as *Worth a Thousand Words, Picture This,* and *Great Books for Babies and Toddlers,* lists of children's picture books are commonplace. The same is true for bibliographic collections of folk and fairy tales. Compiler-specific (Grimm, Andersen), story-specific (Cinderella tales), and country- or culture-specific (Hmong or Mexico) bibliographies exist. None, however, methodically collects deliberate revisions of popular tales.

The concept for this reference book arose in a very conventional manner. A large number of rewritten tales were found when browsing the shelves of an extensive folk and fairy tale collection. These stories differ from other retellings in that the revised text indicates an intent to create a new story from the old. The quantity of silly, fractured revisions of familiar stories is enormous, as are the number of culturally or geographically re-set versions. The total number of all retold folk and fairy tales is so vast that unique and creative revisions are obscured or overlooked in standard reference sources. Often the extent of revision is not apparent from the title, but reveals itself only when read.

This list is edited and annotated for the convenience of users and includes only those titles that exhibit intent to change the original story. Obviously fractured tales (*Cinderfella and the Slam Dunk Contest, Schmoe White and the Seven Dorfs,* and so forth) are included, but all titles whose OCLC record suggested that it might be rewritten in some way were reviewed. Some stories may have minor revisions—

added characters or a change of gender for the main character. Others are set in entirely new cultures and are barely recognizable as a revision of the original. Titles that contained no changes or only minor revisions from the original were not included, nor were books that contained revisions of multiple stories.

The objective of this bibliography is to provide librarians and other professionals with a comprehensive, systematic list of fractured or altered stories that can be used for collection development and to enhance children's services. The stories are indexed by setting or culture, and carry cross-indexed motif labels. These motifs are not intended as subject headings or descriptors and do not categorize the overarching subject of the tales, but list commonly occurring devices that are useful to plan children's services. Because content can depart from standard Aarne-Thompson fairy tale types, many of the titles listed here are not found in traditional fairy tale indexes, or are not described as altered from the original.

An original list of more than 900 titles was developed by searching OCLC databases, online lists of personal and public libraries, and authors who were known to have contributed to the genre. Not all titles were included in the final index. Of 950 titles gathered, just over 300 fell within parameters for inclusion. The vast number and variations of retold tales dictated limiting which original tales were included. Revisions of original tales were limited to authors whose collections are familiar to Americans. Tales collected by the Grimms, Charles Perrault, Joseph Jacobs, Hans Christian Andersen, Asbjørnson and Moe, and Afanas'ev were included, as were the fables of Aesop. Ultimately thirty original tales were identified and the fractured revisions collected and annotated.

The term "fractured" is used here to refer to versions of stories that have changes in the text obvious to the casual reader. A story is considered fractured or altered if it strays enough from an accepted print version to demonstrate intent by the reteller to create a new story from the old. Minimal changes in dialog or description were not considered altered enough to be fractured. Each original story was located in a standard translation commonly available and accepted as an authentic and reliable interpretation of the author's or compiler's work. This is not meant to imply that any of these stories has a definitive version. Authoritative versions were assigned to provide a reference point for revisions, as oral tales have a long and varied history, and similar tales can be found among collections. Versions of Cinderella and Red Riding Hood can be found in both Perrault and Grimm, stories of Tom Thumb in Grimm, Perrault, and Jacobs, and The Pancake in Afanas'ev and Asbjørnson. Other variants include The Pancake, collected by Joseph Jacobs, which is commonly known in the West as The Gingerbread Boy. Standard retellings of this story were not included unless they were significantly different from either variant. Similarly, Stone Soup is retold in *Scandinavian Folk and Fairy Tales* (Booss, 1984) as The Old Woman and the Tramp, a story involving only two characters, but is also known as a conflict between an army and a village. For this bibliography, only versions that revised either story were included.

Exceptions were made for certain revisions. While versions of tales that were essentially the same as the original tale were not collected, those with text that was largely unchanged but whose portrayal demonstrated intent to portray a revised story visually were included. Titles such as *Cinderlily* (Ellwand, 2003), a pictorial of flower photographs, and *Cinderella* (1988), portrayed with canine characters by Diane Goode, use illustration to reinterpret the story and imply revision. Other titles that were included without significantly altered texts were two series, produced by Jump at the Sun and by Winston Derek Publishers. Both series demonstrate intent to present revised stories by portraying the main characters as black. All titles from both series were included to honor the authors' and publishers' intent.

Titles in which the text was unchanged but the author showed a trend toward becoming more fractured in his/her later work were also retained. The author-illustrator team of Lynn and David Roberts is an example. Their earliest work, *Cinderella: An Art Deco Love Story* (Abrams, 2001), would have been excluded because the text, although set in the Roaring Twenties, varied little from Perrault's version. The author-and-illustrator team went on to publish two more titles, however, and each traveled further afield in its revision. By the time the couple published *Little Red: A Fizzingly Good Yarn* (2005), the story was firmly revised for a contemporary audience, including changing the protagonist from female to male. While *Cinderella: An Art Deco Love Story* would not have been included on its own, it is here because it is representative of the author's oeuvre.

The titles included in this bibliography conform to a picture-book format that is appropriate for reading aloud to groups of children or individual children. Titles in reader format, which are meant for children to read themselves and employ simplified vocabulary and sentence structure, were not included. Juvenile books with chapters, and picture books over 48 pages, which are too lengthy for a shared reading encounter, were also omitted.

Each of the twenty-seven tales covered in this bibliography is introduced by a standard version of the story, usually abridged or adapted from well-known sources; in some cases the full story is provided. These synopses will reacquaint readers with the salient points of each tale.

Arrangement of the bibliography is by original tale, with numbered entries listed alphabetically within each division. Each entry provides a bibliographic citation, a summary of the story and how it differs from the original, notes on any added material, and motif and country/culture identifiers. The books listed are illustrated by the author unless otherwise stated. Motifs are provided to cross-reference titles that may be of interest to librarians and other professionals who use these lists to create thematic programs. They refer to common objects or elements that play an overt role in the retold story. The motifs are original to this bibliography and are not intended as subject headings or descriptors or to be used to reference other bibliographies. The same is true for the country/culture designation.

More than just geographic, the country/culture indicator allows titles that are set in cultures without geographical boundaries to be identified and cross-referenced. When assigning country/culture identifiers, the specific country that was mentioned in the title or text was used first. If that was not available, a culture designation was assigned if appropriate. Country/culture designations may not be applicable to each title and are provided only when the revision is based outside an Anglo American setting.

A Bibliography lists sources used in the compilation of this work, and is followed by five indexes: Author, Title, Illustrator, Country/Culture, and Motif. The latter two allow the user who already has a programmatic theme to locate similar titles.

BEAUTY AND THE BEAST

Abridged from *Europa's Fairy Book, Restored and Retold by Joseph Jacobs* (G.P. Putnam's Sons, 1916).

THERE WAS ONCE A MERCHANT WITH A DAUGHTER. When he had to go away he said to her, "What shall I bring you back, my dear?" The daughter replied, "Bring back yourself, Papa."

"Nonsense, child," said her father, "you must say something that I may remember to bring back for you."

"Then bring me back a rose, father," she said.

Well, the merchant went on his journey and when all his work was done he rode off and forgot about the rose till he was near home; so he looked about to find one. Nearby was a lovely rose-bush, and he plucked the most beautiful flower from it. At that moment he heard a crash like thunder, and saw a huge beast.

"Mortal," said the Beast, "who said you could pick my rose?"

"Please, sir," said the merchant, in fear for his life, "I promised my daughter to bring her home a rose and forgot about it till the last moment. Then I saw your beautiful garden and thought you would not miss a single one."

"Thieving is thieving," said the Beast, "whether it be a rose or a diamond."

The merchant fell on his knees and begged for his life for the sake of his daughter who had only him to support her.

"Well, mortal," said the Beast, "I grant your life on one condition: Seven days from now you must bring your daughter and leave her here. Otherwise you place yourself at my disposal."

So the merchant swore, and rode home.

As soon as he got into his house his daughter came rushing to him and he sighed.

Bella said, "Why did you sigh so deeply?"

"Bella, do you love your father?" he asked.

"Of course I do."

"Well, now you have a chance of showing it," and he told her what had occurred.

Bella said, "Oh, Father, it was on account of me that this happened; so I will go. Perhaps he will do me no harm."

So the next day the merchant took Bella to the Beast. When they got there the doors of the house opened, and what do you think they saw there! Nothing. They went up the steps and through the hall into the dining-room and there they saw a table spread with a feast. They waited, thinking that the owner would appear, until the merchant said, "Let's sit down and see what will happen then." When they sat down invisible hands passed them things to eat and to drink, which they did to their hearts' content. And when they arose from the table it disappeared as if it were being carried by invisible servants.

Suddenly the Beast appeared and said to the merchant, "Is this your youngest daughter who is to stop here with me?" And Bella said in a trembling voice, "Yes, sir."

"Well, no harm will come to you." With that he led the merchant out and told him he might come in a week to visit. Then the Beast returned to Bella and said to her, "This house with all that is therein is yours and all you have to do is clap your hands and state your desire and it will come." With that he made a bow and went away.

So Bella lived, and was waited on by invisible servants and had whatever she liked. But she soon got tired of the solitude and was so well treated that she began to seek company in the Beast. So they spoke about the garden and the house and all manner of things, and finally Bella completely lost her fear of him. When her father came to visit and found her happy, he felt much less dread of her fate. So it went on for many days, Bella and the Beast talking every day, till she got to like him. One day the Beast did not come at his usual time, and Bella missed him. So she wandered about the garden trying to find him, calling out his name, but received no reply. At last she came to the bush from which her father had plucked her rose, and there was the Beast lying huddled up without any life. Then Bella was distraught and remembered the kindness the Beast had shown her. She threw herself down by him and said, "Oh, Beast, why did you die? I love you so much."

No sooner had she said this than the hide of the Beast split in two and out came the most handsome young prince. He told her he had been enchanted, and that he could not recover his natural form unless a maiden should, of her own accord, declare that she loved him.

Thereupon the prince married Bella, and they lived happily ever after.

1   COXE, MOLLY. ***Bunny and the Beast.***
Ill. by Pamela Silin-Palmer. Random House, 2001
ISBN: 978-0-375-80468-7
Motifs: Animals (rabbits or hares)
          Animals (dogs)
          Flowers (roses)

In this version, the illustrations are elaborate paintings, with the main characters portrayed as bunnies. The Rabbit Prince has been changed into a bull terrier as punishment for being vain.

2   CRUMP, FRED H. ***A Rose for Zemira: Beauty and the Beast.***
Winston-Derek Publishers, 1988
ISBN: 978-1-55523-151-4
Country/culture: Africa
Motifs: Flowers (roses)
          Monsters, beasts, or magical creatures

In Africa, Zemira is the girl who is held prisoner by the beast named Azor. Every night Azor asks Zemira to marry him, but she replies that she cannot because he is a beast. When her father falls ill, Azor allows Zemira to return home to see him. Upon her return to the castle, Zemira finds Azor close to death and realizes that she does love him after all. When she agrees to marry him, the spell is broken and he turns back into the handsome prince he once was.

3   TUNNELL, MICHAEL O. ***Beauty and the Beastly Children.***
Ill. by John Emil Cymerman. Tambourine Books, 1993
ISBN: 978-0-688-12181-5
Motifs: Monsters, beasts, or magical creatures

This story picks up after Beauty and Auguste marry. Evidently Auguste did not learn his lesson by being turned into a beast, for he has quickly reverted to his vain ways. Beauty gives birth to triplets and they all share the beast's curse. The spell is finally broken for good when Auguste learns to stay home and take care of the children instead of himself.

4   YEP, LAURENCE. ***Dragon Prince: A Chinese Beauty and the Beast Tale.***
Ill. by Kam Mak. HarperCollins, 1997
ISBN: 978-0-06-024381-4
Country/Culture: China
Motifs: Monsters, beasts, or magical creatures
          Clothing (shoes or boots)

Trying to find a bride who is true, a prince disguises himself as a dragon and takes a girl as his betrothed. She loves him as the dragon, so he reveals his true self to her and they marry. When she returns home for a visit, her sisters get jealous and push her into the river. Another sister takes her place and returns to the prince, who, sensing the deception, searches for his true bride until he finds her working for a shoe merchant.

THE BOY WHO CRIED WOLF

As published in *Æsop's Fables: A New Revised Version from Original Sources . . .* (Frank F. Lovell & Company, 1884).

THE SHEPHERD'S BOY AND THE WOLF

A SHEPHERD-BOY, WHO WATCHED A FLOCK OF SHEEP near a village, brought out the villagers three or four times by crying out, "Wolf! Wolf!" and when his neighbors came to help him, laughed at them for their pains. The Wolf, however, did truly come at last. The Shepherd-boy, now really alarmed, shouted in an agony of terror: "Pray, do come and help me; the Wolf is killing the sheep," but no one paid any heed to his cries.

There is no believing a liar, even when he speaks the truth.

5   HARTMAN, BOB.   *The Wolf Who Cried Boy.*
Ill. by Tim Raglin. Putnam, 2002
ISBN: 978-0-399-23578-8
Motifs: Animals (wolves or coyotes)
Little Wolf just wants a change of diet. To avoid eating the routine food his mother has fixed, he cries "Boy!" shortly before dinner is served to cre-

ate a ruckus. Mother and Father Wolf decide to ignore him and a whole troop of young boy scouts comes walking through the woods and into the cave.

6   LEVINE, GAIL CARSON. *Betsy Who Cried Wolf.*
Ill. by Scott Nash. HarperCollins, 2002
ISBN: 978-0-06-028763-4
Motifs: Gender role reversal
        Animals (wolves or coyotes)
Zimmo the wolf tries to outsmart shepherd Betsy by appearing and disappearing and ruining her reputation for reliability. When Betsy sees that Zimmo is just a skinny hungry old wolf, she gives him her lunch and they realize that he could be a great sheep herder too.

7   ROCCO, JOHN. *Wolf! Wolf!*
Hyperion Books for Children, 2007
ISBN: 978-1-4231-0012-6
Motifs: Animals (wolves or coyotes)
        Animals (goats)
The wolf, too old to chase goats anymore, makes a bargain with the boy who keeps getting into trouble with the villagers. The wolf tells the boy that he won't eat him if he gives the wolf one of his goats. When it comes time for the wolf to eat the goat, he realizes that the goat's grazing is allowing vegetables to grow in his garden. Knowing that a lifetime of vegetables is more valuable than one meal of goat meat, the wolf decides to keep the goat instead of eating him.

8   ROSS, TONY. *The Boy Who Cried Wolf.*
Dial Books for Young Readers, 1985
ISBN: 978-0-8037-0193-9
Motifs: Animals (wolves or coyotes)
Willy has a habit of crying "wolf!" whenever there is something he doesn't want to do. So when the wolf actually does chase Willy, no one believes him. Luckily for Willy, the wolf finds the villagers watching the scene to be tastier treats than Willy might be.

9   WATTENBERG, JANE.   *Never Cry Woof! A Dog-U-Drama.*
Scholastic, 2005
ISBN: 978-0-439-21675-3
Motifs: Animals (wolves or coyotes)
        Animals (dogs)
A dog story full of puns and wordplay. Bix the dog cries wolf so many
times that the other dogs won't help him when the wolf really does show
up. When Bix leaves the field to complain about the other dogs' lack of
interest, the wolves eat the sheep he left behind.

THE BRAVE LITTLE TAILOR

A much longer version of this story with the title "The Gallant Tailor" is found in *Household Stories by the Brothers Grimm* (Macmillan and Company, 1886). In that account, the tailor buys jelly from an old woman while he works, and the jelly attracts the flies he kills. The tailor sets out to tell the world of his accomplishment, but encounters a giant along the way. After fooling the giant several times, the tailor goes to a kingdom and demands to work for the king's army. In an effort to rid himself of the fellow, the king sends the tailor out on three tasks, believing each time that he would fail. Finally, the king agrees to let the tailor marry his daughter. After the marriage, the tailor talks in his sleep and reveals his lowly birth. The princess demands that he be deposed, but the tailor uses his cunning again to fool her guards into fearing him. The version below is abridged from *English Fairy Tales Collected by Joseph Jacobs* (Third edition, revised. G.P. Putnam's Son', 1902).

THE BRAVE LITTLE TAILOR (JOHNNY GLOKE)

JOHNNY GLOKE WAS A TAILOR BY TRADE, but had grown tired of his tailoring. He wanted to do something that would lead to honor and fame. One warm day he was annoyed by the flies around his bare ankles. He slapped at them with force and killed several. On counting them he was overjoyed at his success, and he sang:

"Well done! Johnny Gloke, Kilt fifty flies at one stroke."

Now he would get his honor and fame. So he took up a rusty old sword and set out in search of adventure. After a long bit, he came to a country that was troubled by two giants. He learned that the King had offered the hand of his daughter in marriage to the man who rid them of this scourge. John's heart rose to the deed, and he offered his services to the King. The King agreed, and John set out to the wood where the giants lived. He stopped to think of a plan when he saw the giants

9

coming. My they were big ones! They had huge heads and long tusks for teeth. Johnny hid himself in the hollow of a tree. Feeling safe, he peeped out and watched the two. Then he picked up a pebble, and threw it at one, striking him in the head. In his pain, the giant turned on his companion and blamed him. The other denied the charge. John kept still and watched for another opportunity to strike. He found it, and another pebble went to the giant's head. The injured giant fell on his companion in fury, and the two fought till they were tired out. They sat down to breathe and recover themselves.

One of them said, "Yesterday the King's army was not able to take us, but today I fear an old woman with a rope would be too much."

"If that is so," said Johnny Gloke as he sprang from his hiding-place, "What do you say to Johnny Gloke with his old rusty sword?" And he fell upon them, cut off their heads, and returned in triumph. He married the King's daughter and for a time lived in peace and happiness. But he never told how he had killed the giants.

Some time later a rebellion broke out. Because of his earlier exploits, Johnny was chosen to quell the rebellion. He was afraid, but he could not refuse and lose his great name. He mounted the fiercest horse that ever saw sun, and set out on his task. He was not accustomed to riding, and he soon lost control. The steed galloped off at full speed in the direction of the rebels. It passed under the wayside gallows, which fell on the horse's neck. Still the horse ran forward at a furious pace toward the rebels. On seeing this strange sight approaching them the rebels were seized with terror, and cried out, "There comes Johnny Gloke who killed the two giants! He has a gallows on his horse's neck to hang us all." They broke their ranks and fled, never stopping till they reached their homes. Thus Johnny Gloke was victorious a second time. So in due time he came to the throne and lived a long and happy life as King.

10   COMPTON, KENN, AND JOANNE COMPTON. *Jack the Giant Chaser: An Appalachian Tale.*

Holiday House, 1993

ISBN: 978-0-8234-0998-3

Country/Culture: Appalachia

Motifs: Monsters, beasts, or magical creatures

This Jack impresses the mayor when he kills seven fish with one stone. The mayor believes Jack is unusually brave and sends him to dispatch a giant. Instead of actually fighting, Jack tells the giant tales of what he is going to do to him, thereby scaring the giant off.

11   JOHNSON, PAUL BRETT.   *Fearless Jack.*
Margaret K. McElderry Books, 2001
ISBN: 978-0-689-83296-3
Country/Culture: Appalachia
Motifs: Monsters, beasts, or magical creatures
Jack is out fishing by his mountain home when he inadvertently kills ten flies with one blow. He meets up with a local sheriff who believes the deed to be greater than it was. The sheriff sends Jack to vanquish wild varmints who are terrorizing the town. Through cunning rather than strength, Jack defeats a wild boar, a grizzly bear, and a unicorn with an attitude problem. Includes author's note on the origin of Jack tales.

12   OSBORNE, MARY POPE.   *The Brave Little Seamstress.*
Ill. by Giselle Potter. Atheneum, 2002
ISBN: 978-0-689-84486-7
Motifs: Gender role reversal
        Monsters, beasts, or magical creatures
In this story, the main character is a woman. She inadvertently kills ten flies with one blow and announces the feat, which is inflated in its retelling. Because of this, she is chosen to battle wild beasts that are terrorizing the town. Instead of using might, she defeats each by using her wits.

THE BREMEN TOWN MUSICIANS

Abridged from *Household Stories* by the Brothers Grimm (Macmillan and Company, 1886).

THERE WAS ONCE AN ASS WHO HAD WORKED for his master many years, but whose strength had begun to fail. His master thought of turning him out, so the ass ran away, taking the road to Bremen to become a town musician. Along the way he found a hound lying by the side of the road panting, as if he had been running.

"What are you so out of breath about?" said the ass.

"Oh dear!" said the dog, "I am old, and can't hunt, so my master was going to have me killed, I made my escape, but now what do I do?"

"I will tell you what," said the ass, "I am going to Bremen to become a town musician. You may as well go with me, and take up music too."

The dog agreed, and they walked together. Shortly they came to a cat sitting in the road, looking dismal.

"What is the matter with you?" asked the ass.

"Now that I am old, my teeth are blunt so my mistress wanted to drown me. I ran off, but what is to become of me?" answered the cat.

"Go with us to Bremen," said the ass, "and become a town musician. You understand serenading."

The cat thought this was a good idea, and went with them. Then the three travelers passed a cock perched on a gate crowing his heart out.

"Cock, what is the matter?" asked the ass.

"I have foretold good weather for my Lady for many years, but company is coming. My mistress has told the cook that I will be made into soup."

"You should go with us, Chanticleer," said the ass. "We are going to Bremen to become town musicians. You have a powerful voice, and can join in."

So together the four continued down the road.

Towards evening they spied a light from a cottage in the woods, and thought they could spend the night. They set off in that direction until they came to a house. The ass, being the biggest, went to the window, and looked in.

"What do you see?" asked the dog.

"What do I see?" answered the ass. "I see a table set with food and drink, but robbers are sitting at it and making themselves comfortable."

"That table would just suit us," said the cock.

"Yes, indeed," said the ass. So they devised a plan to get the robbers out of the house. The ass placed his forefeet on the window-sill, the dog got on the ass's back, the cat on the top of the dog, and the cock flew up and perched on the cat's head. Then they all began to perform their music. The ass brayed, the dog barked, the cat mewed, and the cock crowed, and they all burst into the house. The robbers, thinking it was a goblin, fled at the dreadful sound. Then the four companions sat down at the table, and feasted on the remains of the meal. When they had finished, each found a sleeping-place to his liking. The ass laid down on the dunghill, the dog behind the door, the cat on the hearth, and the cock in the cockloft, and they soon fell fast asleep.

When midnight drew near, the robbers saw the lights go out from afar. The captain said that he thought that they had run away needlessly, and told one to go reconnoiter. So the one went, and he found everything quiet. He went into the kitchen to light a fire. But he mistook the glowing eyes of the cat for burning coals, and he held a match to them. The cat flew into his face, spitting and scratching. The robber cried out in terror, and ran to the back door. The dog who was lying there bit his leg, and as he rushed outside by the dunghill the ass struck out and gave him a great kick. The cock, who had wakened with the noise, cried out, "Cock-a-doodle-doo!"

The robber ran back to his captain, and said, "In that house there is a witch! I felt her breath and her long nails on my face! By the door was a man who stabbed me in the leg with a knife; and in the yard there lies a ghost, who beat me; and on the roof there sits a judge who cried, 'Bring that rogue here!' And so I ran away!"

The robbers never again ventured to that house, and the four Bremen town musicians found themselves so comfortable that they stayed there forever.

13   DAVIS, DONALD. *Jack and the Animals: An Appalachian Folktale.*
Ill. by Kitty Harvill. August House Little Folk, 1995
ISBN: 978-0-87483-413-0
Country/Culture: Appalachia
Motifs: Animals

In this story set in the mountains, the animals are led by a boy named Jack who is going in search of his fortune. Approaching the shack of thieves, the animals hide to keep from being seen. When the cat is discovered, all the other animals help to create a havoc that makes the thieves believe that the house is haunted.

14   PRICE, KATHY. *The Bourbon Street Musicians.*
Ill. by Andrew Glass. Clarion Books, 2002
ISBN: 978-0-618-04076-6
Country/Culture: New Orleans
Motifs: Animals
          Monsters, beasts, or magical creatures
          Music (jazz)

These animals are on their way through the bayou to become New Orleans musicians when they come upon a shack occupied by roughnecks. They begin to sing in order to be invited in, but are mistaken for a loup-garou (werewolf) and the thieves flee the house, leaving it for the animals to occupy. Includes a glossary of Creole, French, and southern slang words.

CINDERELLA

The story below is adapted from *The Tales of Mother Goose as First Collected by Charles Perrault in 1696* (D.C. Heath & Co. 1901), but many versions exist. In the Grimm account ("Aschenputtel" in *Household Stories*), the main character speaks with the animals around her and they become her guardians against the stepmother's wickedness. Three times Cinderella asks to attend the ball, and the stepmother assigns her impossible tasks, and each time the animals help her complete it, but she still cannot attend. After the others depart, the birds bring Cinderella the gown and slippers, and there is no mention of a coach. At the conclusion, the stepsisters both chop off part of their feet to make the slipper fit, but each time the birds tell the prince of his mistake. On the day of the wedding, the stepsisters arrive at the castle only to have their eyes pecked out by these same birds, and they live as blind beggars for the rest of their lives.

CINDERELLA, OR THE LITTLE GLASS SLIPPER

ONCE THERE WAS A GENTLEMAN WHO MARRIED a proud, haughty woman with two daughters exactly like her. The gentleman had also a young daughter of his own, but she was good and sweet as her mother had been.

Because she made her daughters appear worse, the stepmother could not bear this girl. So she gave her the worst work in the house and made her sleep aloft. Each day when she finished her work, she was so covered with dirt and ashes that the stepsisters called the girl Cinderella.

One day an invitation arrived at the house. The prince was having a ball, and all ladies were invited. The stepsisters were delighted and immediately got ready. They chose dresses and fussed about their hair and figures. All the while Cinderella helped them, but they gave her no thought. When they departed, Cinderella ran to the garden and cried.

Her fairy godmother appeared and asked Cinderella why she wept.

"I want to go to the ball," she sobbed.

17

"So you shall," said her godmother, "Bring me a pumpkin."

Cinderella brought it and her godmother struck it with her wand. The pumpkin was turned into a gilded coach.

Then she asked for six mice and tapped each with her wand, and turned it into fine mouse-colored steed. The three coachmen were changed from rats, and six footmen from lizards.

The fairy said, "How do you like it?"

"It's lovely," she cried, "but must I go in these rags?"

"I almost forgot!" Her godmother touched her with the wand and turned her clothes into gold and silver, decked with jewels. Finally, she was given the prettiest glass slippers in the whole world.

As Cinderella got into the carriage, her godmother warned her to be home by midnight, when everything would return to its original form. Cinderella promised, and she rode away happier than she had ever been.

When she got to the castle, everyone stopped to stare at the beautiful princess. The prince took her hand to greet her, and scarcely let it go the rest of the evening. They danced and talked and had a wonderful time. When they sat down to eat, the prince was so enamored with Cinderella that he didn't take one bite, and the King himself said he had never seen so lovely a creature.

Too soon, Cinderella heard the clock strike quarter to twelve. She said her goodbyes and hastily left the castle.

When she arrived home, she found her godmother and thanked her. Then she asked to go again the next night, as the prince had invited her. The godmother agreed to this and left as the stepsisters returned. They told Cinderella of the beautiful princess who had captivated everyone, but Cinderella just smiled and listened.

The next day the two sisters returned to the ball, as did Cinderella. Again, the prince never left Cinderella's side, and behaved as if no one else existed in the world. Midnight came too soon, and this time the young lady forgot her godmother's orders. When she saw that she was late, she fled as a deer into the wood. The prince followed, but one of her glass slippers was all that was all he found

The next day the king sent out a proclamation that the prince intended to find the girl, and every lady in the kingdom was asked to try on the slipper. Whoever it fit would be the prince's bride.

When the slipper was brought to the house, the two sisters did all they possibly could to make it fit, but their feet were just too big. Cinderella saw this and said, "Let me try."

The stepsisters laughed, but the king's servant with the slipper agreed.

Cinderella to sat down and put the shoe on her little foot. It fit her foot as if it was made of wax. The sisters were astonished, but when Cinderella took the other shoe from her pocket, they knew the truth. They bowed and begged her forgiveness for their ill treatment. Cinderella embraced them and promised to love them always.

So it was that the girls went to the castle to meet Cinderella's intended. After they were married, Cinderella, who was as good as she was beautiful, gave her two sisters a home in the palace, and married them to two lords of the court.

15   ADAMS, EDWARD BEN.   *The Korean Cinderella.*
Ill. by Dong Ho Choi. Seoul International Pub. Co., 1982
Country/Culture: Korea
Motifs: Clothing (shoes or boots)
      Space

A version of Kongjee and Patjee published in Korea. This time the wish-granter is the Weaving Maid from Beyond the Milky Way, who weaves Kongjee a new dress and makes her beautiful slippers to attend a wedding. A slipper is retrieved by a passing official who goes to the wedding to track down its owner. Text in Korean and English. Includes author's note. Korean Folkstory for Children, series 5.

16   AUCH, MARY JANE.   *Chickerella.*
Ill. by Herm Auch. Holiday House, 2005
ISBN: 978-0-8234-1804-6
Motifs: Clothing (shoes or boots)
      Birds (chickens)

Chickerella lays glass eggs. She wants to go to the Fowl Ball to see all the dresses. Fairy Goosemother tells her to go. As she leaves the ball she lays an egg on the steps. The prince finds her but Chickerella doesn't want to marry him and he says he wasn't looking for a bride, just had the ball to see the fashion. Fairy Goosemother reappears and the three start their own fashion line.

17   BOURGEOIS, KAREN M.   *Trollerella.*
Ill. by Ethan Long. Holiday House, 2006
ISBN: 978-0-8234-1918-0
Motifs: Monsters, beasts, or magical creatures
      Teeth
      Clothing (shoes or boots)
      Jewelry

Trollerella lives under the bridge, but finds an invitation to the ball. The tooth fairy promises to make her beautiful for one night. When the prince finds her oversized glass slipper, Trollerella worries that he won't love her, so the tooth fairy casts a spell on him to fall in love with her. The tiny engagement ring fits perfectly on the wart on her nose.

18   BUEHNER, CARALYN.   *Fanny's Dream.*
Ill. by Mark Buehner. Dial Books for Young Readers, 1996
ISBN: 978-0-8037-1496-0
Motifs: Clothing

When Fanny's fairy godmother doesn't turn up to grant her wishes, Fanny marries Heber the neighbor boy. They settle down to a life that includes more than a few hardships. But when the fairy godmother finally shows up years later, Fanny decides that her dreams have already come true.

19   BURTON, ELIZABETH.   *Cinderfella and the Slam Dunk Contest.*
Ill. by Lynn Offerdahl. Branden Pub. Co., 1994
ISBN: 978-0-8283-1966-9
Country/Culture: African American
Motifs: Sports (basketball)
          Clothing (shoes or boots)
          Gender role reversal

Cinderfella is a mean boy and as punishment doesn't get to go to a basketball game. He promises his fairy godfather, Michael Jordan, that he will change his ways if he can go to the event. With the help of magic Sparkling Turbo Air Pumps, Cinderfella wins the contest, but loses a sneaker as he leaves.

20   CLIMO, SHIRLEY.   *The Egyptian Cinderella.*
Ill. by Ruth Heller. Crowell, 1989
ISBN: 978-0-690-04822-3
Country/Culture: Egypt
Motifs: Clothing (shoes or boots)
          Birds (falcons)

Rhodophis is a slave in Egypt with blond hair, green eyes, and sunburned skin. Her master sees her dancing and favors her with a pair of slippers of leather and gold. A falcon steals one and drops it in Pharaoh's lap. When Pharaoh finds Rhodophis, the servants argue that she is not Egyptian. Pharaoh says that her eyes are green like the Nile, her hair as feathery as papyrus, and her skin the pink of a lotus flower. Includes author's note.

21   CLIMO, SHIRLEY.   *The Irish Cinderlad.*
Ill. by Loretta Krupinski. HarperCollins, 1996
ISBN: 978-0-06-024396-8

Country/Culture: Ireland
Motifs: Clothing (shoes or boots)
Animals (bulls)
Monsters, beasts, or magical creatures
Dragons

Becan is a small shepherd boy with enormous feet. With the help of a magic bull, he is able to steal a giant's boots and slay a dragon. The princess, whom he saves from the dragon, can track him down by his large boots. Includes author's note.

22   CLIMO, SHIRLEY.   *The Korean Cinderella.*
Ill. by Ruth Heller. HarperCollins, 1993
ISBN: 978-0-06-020432-7
Country/Culture: Korea
Motifs: Clothing (shoes or boots)
Monsters, beasts, or magical creatures

Pear Blossom is the only child of elderly parents. When her mother dies, her new mother Omoni (Korean for mother), and Peony, her daughter, nickname Pear Blossom "Pigling." Instead of a single fairy, a series of togkabis (magical creatures) help Pear Blossom complete her tasks so that she can go to the festival. On the way, she loses one of her straw sandals, which is found by a magistrate. Includes author's note on the story and illustrator's note on the images depicted.

23   CLIMO, SHIRLEY.   *The Persian Cinderella.*
Ill. by Robert Florczak. HarperCollins, 1999
ISBN: 978-0-06-026763-6
Country/Culture: Iran
Motifs: Jewelry
Stars

When Settareh (named for the star birthmark on her cheek) and her sisters are given money to buy cloth for the New Year Festival, Settareh spends hers on a small blue jug. The jug is occupied by a fairy, who gives her a new dress and diamond anklets for the festival. Settareh flees the festival and loses an anklet on her way back. When the prince finds her, a wedding date is set, but the sisters attempt to thwart the marriage by using the jug fairy against her. Includes author's note on the origin of the story.

24   COBURN, JEWELL REINHART. *Angkat: The Cambodian Cinderella.*
Ill. by Edmund Flotte. Shen's Books, 1998
ISBN: 978-1-885008-09-1
Country/Culture: Cambodia
Motifs: Clothing (shoes or boots)
        Fish
        Birds

Angkat befriends a fish. Kantok, her stepsister, is jealous and kills it. The Spirit of Virtue appears to Angkat and tells her to put the bones under her pillow. A pair of golden slippers appears, and a black bird steals one. The bird gives it to the prince, who is determined to find its owner. Sadly, after they marry, Angkat's family kills her to have Kantok take her place. Includes author's note.

25   COBURN, JEWELL REINHART. *Domitila: A Cinderella Tale from the Mexican Tradition.*
Ill. by Connie McLennan. Shen's Books, 2000
ISBN: 978-1-885008-13-8
Country/Culture: Mexico
Motifs: Food

When her mother gets ill, Domitila is sent to the governor's mansion to work. There, the governor's son falls in love with her, but when she finds that her mother has died, Domitila flees the mansion, leaving only a piece of finely tooled leather behind. Includes Mexican proverbs with English translations on each spread. Includes publisher's note, recipe for nopales, and a glossary of Spanish terms.

26   COBURN, JEWELL REINHART. *Jouanah: A Hmong Cinderella.*
Ill. by Tzexa Cherta Lee. Shen's Books, 1996
ISBN: 978-1-885008-01-5
Country/Culture: Hmong
Motifs: Clothing (shoes or boots)
        Holidays (Chinese New Year)

The wish-granter is the spirit of Jouanah's dead mother, and she outfits her daughter for the New Year's festival. After the festival, Jouanah is found by the handsome Shee-Nang, son of a village elder. The stepmother tries to sabotage the engagement, but doesn't succeed in splitting them up.

27   COHLENE, TERRI.   *Little Firefly.*
Ill. by Charles Reasoner. Rourke Corporation, 1990
ISBN: 978-0-86593-005-6
Country/Culture: Native American (Algonquin)
Motifs: Clothing
           Stars

After their mother's death, Firefly is tormented by her sisters. In a dream, her mother tells Little Firefly that she will find happiness in the forest. Firefly makes herself a new dress from birch bark and weeds, and goes down the river. She sees the smoke from a campfire and follows it. At the campsite she meets the sister of the Invisible One, and offers to work for them. When he returns from hunting, Firefly can see the Invisible One, and he recognizes that this makes her special. His sister makes her beautiful and the two are married. Includes 14 pages of information on Algonquin life and culture.

28   COLE, BABETTE.   *Prince Cinders.*
Putnam, 1988
ISBN: 978-0-399-21502-5
Motifs: Monsters, beasts, or magical creatures
           Animals (monkeys)
           Gender role reversal
           Transportation (buses)

Prince Cinders is "small, spotty, scruffy, and skinny." When a well-meaning but incompetent fairy tries to make him "big and hairy" like his brothers, she turns him into a giant monkey. Cinders can't get into the dance hall because he is too big. He goes to the bus stop and meets the princess. She is at first afraid of him, but then he transforms back to himself and she believes that Cinders has saved her from the giant ape. Running from the scene, Cinders leaves his giant pants behind, which the princess uses to locate him.

29   COLLINS, SHEILA HÉBERT.   *Cendrillon: A Cajun Cinderella.*
Ill. by Patrick Soper. Pelican, 1998
ISBN: 978-1-56554-326-3
Country/Culture: Cajun
Motifs: Clothing (shoes or boots)
           Holidays (Mardi Gras)

Set in New Orleans, this version uses French words and phrases. Cendrillon lives in a shotgun house and is friends with the local animals:

Crawfish, Alligator, Crab, and Pelican. They help her make a dress for Mardi Gras. The fairy godmother appears and helps her get to the masquerade ball where she meets Rex, the King of Mardi Gras. The two dance until midnight, when Cendrillon must return to the swamp. When he finds her again, Rex and Cendrillon quickly hop a streetcar to the French Quarter and get married at St. Louis Cathedral. Includes pronunciation guide and definitions for French words on each page. Includes a recipe for red beans and rice.

30   COMPTON, JOANNE. *Ashpet: An Appalachian Tale.*
Ill. by Kenn Compton. Holiday House, 1994
ISBN: 978-0-8234-1106-1
Country/Culture: Appalachia
Motifs: Clothing (shoes or boots)

Ashpet is the servant to an old widow and her daughters. Each summer there is a big church meeting, but this year the fire goes out in the church the night before. The widow sends Ashpet to get fire from the old grandmother. Ashpet is kind to her and Granny gives her the fire. After the others leave, Granny magically cleans the house for Ashpet and provides her with a dress and red shoes to wear to church. The doctor's son falls in love with Ashpet at the church and uses one of the red shoes she leaves behind to find her. Includes author's note.

31   DALY, JUDE. *Fair, Brown and Trembling : An Irish Cinderella Story.*
Farrar, Straus and Giroux, 2000
ISBN: 978-0-374-32247-2
Country/Culture: Ireland
Motifs: Clothing (shoes or boots)

Fair, Brown, and Trembling are three sisters. Trembling is bullied by the other two. When Fair and Brown go to church, an old woman admonishes Trembling for not going. Trembling explains the situation and the old woman magically produces a white gown and shamrock-green slippers. After weeks of appearing like this, princes from all over the country come to see her at the church. The Prince of Emania steals her shoe and uses it to locate her after the mass.

32   DE LA PAZ, MYRNA J. *Abadeha: The Philippine Cinderella.*
Ill. by You-shan Tang. Shen's Books, 2001
ISBN: 978-1-885008-17-6
Country/Culture: Philippines

Motifs: Jewelry
　　　Clothing

After a series of abusive incidents with her stepmother, the Spirit of the Forest gives Abadeha an enchanted tree that flowers with all sorts of beautiful jewelry and clothing. Abadeha keeps it a secret from the wicked stepmother. One day the son of the chieftain of the island happens upon the tree and takes a ring from it, which he puts on his finger. The ring becomes painful on his hand, but he cannot remove it. He has a vision that the girl who can remove the ring will be his bride.

33　　DE PAOLA, TOMIE. *Adelita: A Mexican Cinderella Story.*
Putnam, 2002
ISBN: 978-0-399-23866-6
Country/Culture: Mexico
Motifs: Clothing

Adelita lives in the attic and cooks and cleans for her stepmother and stepsisters. A local ranch owner throws a party for his son, Javier. Adelita is visited by her former nanny, Esperanza, who shows her a trunk that holds Adelita's mother's fiesta clothing. Dressed in a traditional embroidered dress and shawl, Adelita goes to the fiesta and meets Javier. She hangs her shawl in her window when she returns and this is how Javier finds her. Includes translated Spanish phrases.

34　　EDWARDS, PAMELA DUNCAN. *Dinorella: A Prehistoric Fairy Tale.*
Ill. by Henry Cole. Hyperion Books for Children, 1997
ISBN: 978-0-7868-0309-5
Motifs: Dinosaurs
　　　Jewelry

Dinorella is told by her sisters, Dora and Doris, that she is "too dowdy" and "too dull" to go to the dance. Fairydactyl gives her dazzling dinosaur diamonds to wear. Dinorella rescues dashing Duke Dudley from the deadly deinonychus by throwing one of her diamonds at him.

35　　ELLWAND, DAVID. *Cinderlily: A Floral Fairy Tale in Three Acts.*
Ill. by Christine Tagg. Candlewick Press, 2003
ISBN: 978-0-7636-2328-9
Motifs: Flowers

The illustrations in this version are all photographs of flowers. Cinderlily is depicted as a faded orchid who loses a petal at the Sultan's ball. The stepsisters are pansies, and all the background details are constructed of flora and fauna. The text is told in rhyme.

36 GOODE, DIANE. *Cinderella: The Dog and Her Little Glass Slipper.*
Blue Sky Press, 2000
ISBN: 978-0-439-07166-6
Motifs: Animals (dogs)
 Clothing (shoes or boots)

This version stays close to the original, but the characters are portrayed as dogs in the illustrations. It also depicts two balls that Cinderella attends. At the first, she meets the prince and he invites her to come to another. She manages to leave this first ball on time. At the second ball she loses track of time and leaves one of her glass slippers behind.

37 GRANOWSKY, ALVIN. *That Awful Cinderella.*
Ill. by Rhonda Childress. Steck-Vaughn, 1993
ISBN: 978-0-8114-2204-8
Motifs: Clothing (shoes or boots)

This edition has the original tale in the first part; then the book is turned over to read the stepsister's story. In the version narrated by the stepsister, Cinderella is portrayed as selfish, greedy, and conniving. Part of the publisher's Point of View series.

38 HAN, OKI S. *Kongi and Potgi: A Cinderella Story from Korea.*
Ill. by Stephanie Haboush Plunkett. Dial Books, 1994
ISBN: 978-0-8037-1571-4
Country/Culture: Korea
Motifs: Clothing (shoes or boots)
 Angels
 Animals (bulls)

Kongi is the abused girl and Potgi is her spoiled stepsister. The plot of this version remains essentially the same as the European, but the setting has changed to ancient Korea and instead of a fairy godmother there are angels who provide magical slippers. Includes author's note and some translated words.

39   HAYES, JOE.   *Estrellita de Oro / Little Gold Star: A Cinderella Cuento.*

Ill. by Gloria Perez and Lucia Perez. Cinco Puntos Press, 2000
ISBN: 978-0-938317-49-4
Country/Culture: Hispanic
Motifs: Stars
      Birds (hawks)

Arcia is the daughter of a shepherd. When she goes to clean and weave the wool of her sheep, a hawk swoops out of the sky and steals it from her. The hawk tells her to look up at the sky, and a small gold star fastens itself to Arcia's forehead. When her stepsisters try to do the same thing they get a donkey ear and a green horn on their heads. It is the gold star that the prince identifies her by after she flees his party. Includes bilingual text.

40   HICKOX, REBECCA.   *The Golden Sandal: A Middle Eastern Cinderella.*

Ill. by Will Hillenbrand. Holiday House, 1998
ISBN: 978-0-8234-1331-7
Country/Culture: Middle East
Motifs: Clothing (shoes or boots)
      Fish

Maha befriends a small magical fish who provides her with what she asks. She asks to go to a local wedding, and the fish gives Maha a silk gown, pearl comb, and gold sandals. Leaving the wedding party in a rush, she loses a sandal in a stream. It is found by the brother of the bride. Maha's step-mother tries to spoil the match, but her attempts backfire and Maha and Tariq live happily ever after. Includes author's note and illustrator's note.

41   HUGHES, SHIRLEY.   *Ella's Big Chance: A Jazz-Age Cinderella.*

Simon & Schuster, 2004
ISBN: 978-0-689-87399-7
Motifs: Music (jazz)
      Clothing (shoes or boots)

Set in the 1920s, this version has an added character. Buttons is a young apprentice in the dress shop owned by Cinderella and her father, making deliveries and doing odd jobs. The story follows the traditional story line with the Fairy Godmother (along with Buttons) helping her get to the ball; however, when the Duke of Arc locates Cinderella she decides she is in love with Buttons instead. They leave town to open a dress shop of their own.

42   JACKSON, ELLEN B. *Cinder Edna.*

Ill. by Kevin O'Malley. Lothrop, Lee & Shepard, 1994
ISBN: 978-0-688-12322-2
Motifs: Clothing (shoes or boots)

Cinder Edna lives next door to Cinderella. She isn't beautiful but she's funny, spunky, and strong. She thinks the prince is boring so when Cinderella is off dancing with him, Edna talks with the prince's younger brother. Edna and Cinderella leave at midnight, but the brother uses a phone book to find Edna while the prince is trying shoes on all the girls of the kingdom to find Cinderella. The two couples are married in a double ceremony. Cinderella lives a boring but pretty life and Cinder Edna lives happily ever after.

43   JAFFE, NINA. *Way Meat Loves Salt: A Cinderella Tale from the Jewish Tradition.*

Ill. by Louise August. Henry Holt, 1998
ISBN: 978-0-8050-4384-6
Country/Culture: Jewish
Motifs: Clothing (shoes or boots)

Mireleh is thrown out of her house. Elijah the prophet gives her a magic stick and sends her to the home of a rabbi who gives her a bed in the attic. Mireleh uses the stick to make a dress and shoes so she can attend a wedding. The rabbi's son falls in love with her and puts tar and pitch on the front step so her shoe will stick to it and he can find her. Includes author's note. Words and sheet music for Mazel Tov!

44   JOHNSTON, TONY. *Bigfoot Cinderrrrella.*

Ill. by James Warhola. Putnam, 1998
ISBN: 978-0-399-23021-9
Motifs: Monsters, beasts, or magical creatures
        Clothing (shoes or boots)
        Ecology

Being big and stinky is good, while picking wildflowers is a no-no. Rrrrrella meets her beary godfather (a grizzly) who gives her the bark clogs she needs to go to the fun-fest held by the Bigfoot prince. Once there, she dunks the prince in a log-rolling contest, and he immediately falls for her. At the wedding in the old-growth forest, the stepmother and stepsisters are allowed to attend if they promise to follow three rules: no pick flowers, no pull tree, no kick royal family. Includes a glossary of terms.

45 JUNGMAN, ANN. *Cinderella and the Hot Air Balloon.*
Ill. by Russell Ayto. Frances Lincoln, 1992
ISBN: 978-0-7112-0726-4
Motifs: Balloons (hot air)

Cinderella is a free spirit who likes to climb trees and hang out with the servants. When it is time for the ball, Cinderella insists her fairy godmother take all the servants out for a night of fun. They have such a great party that the ball guests join them. That is how Cinderella meets Prince Charming. In the end they both want to escape the wealth and fame, so the fairy godmother changes the pumpkin coach into a hot air balloon and they sail away.

46 KETTEMAN, HELEN. *Bubba the Cowboy Prince: A Fractured Texas Tale.*
Ill. by James Warhola. Scholastic, 1997
ISBN: 978-0-590-25506-6
Country/Culture: Western
Motifs: Cowboys
        Animals (cows)
        Clothing (shoes or boots)

Bubba is the maltreated brother of Dwayne and Milton. Miz Lurleen, the prettiest and richest ranch owner in the county, throws a ball to find her perfect ranch hand. With the help of his fairy godcow, Bubba is able to attend Miz Lurleen's ball and win her affection.

47 KHA, DANG MANH, AND ANN NOLAN CLARK. *In the Land of Small Dragon: A Vietnamese Folktale.*
Ill. by Tony Chen. Viking, 1979
ISBN: 978-0-670-39697-9
Country/Culture: Vietnam
Motifs: Clothing (shoes or boots)

A lengthy version of the Tam and Cam story. Cam is Tam's stepsister. A magic fish asks Tam to care for the smaller fish in the pond every day. Cam and her mother catch and eat the magic fish out of jealousy. Tam buries the bones, and when she digs them up she finds a pair of shoes. A crow takes one to the Crown Prince and he marries Tam when he finds that the shoe is hers.

48   KURTZ, JOHN.   *Cinderella.*
Jump at the Sun/Hyperion Books for Children, 2004
ISBN: 978-0-7868-0955-4
Country/Culture: African American
Motifs: Clothing (shoes or boots)

In this standard retelling of the original story, the characters have been changed in the illustrations to be African American. In this version, a rabbit, five mice, and a pumpkin become the coachman, horses, and coach. Part of the Jump at the Sun Fairy-tale Classics series.

49   LATTIMORE, DEBORAH NOURSE.   *Cinderhazel: The Cinderella of Halloween.*
Scholastic, 1996
ISBN: 978-0-590-20232-9
Motifs: Holidays (Halloween)

Cinderhazel is a witch named Hermione who loves to play in the dirt. So much so that her stepsisters don't want to get near her. But what the stepsisters don't know is that Prince Awful is actually Prince Awfully Filthy, so he and Cinderhazel are a perfect match.

50   LOUIE, AI-LING.   *Yeh-Shen: A Cinderella Story from China.*
Ill. by Ed Young. Philomel Books, 1982
ISBN: 978-0-399-20900-0
Country/Culture: China
Motifs: Fish
           Clothing (shoes or boots)

Yeh-Shen has only one friend, a fish that she raised from birth. When her jealous stepmother finds out about the fish, she kills it for food. Yeh-Shen retrieves the bones of the fish from the garbage heap, and their magical powers give her a gown of azure blue and a cloak of feathers to wear to the spring festival. She loses a tiny gold slipper and tries to retrieve it from the king, whereupon she is stopped as a thief, but discovered to be the true owner.

51   LOWELL, SUSAN.   *Cindy Ellen: A Wild Western Cinderella.*
Ill. by Jane Manning. HarperCollins, 2000
ISBN: 978-0-06-027447-4
Country/Culture: Western
Motifs: Clothing (shoes or boots)
           Cowboys

Cindy Ellen lives on a ranch with her stepmother and stepsisters. A rich rancher decides to throw a rodeo and square dance that Cindy Ellen cannot attend. Her fairy godmother appears with a gold pistol and shoots Cindy Ellen with fairy dust, dressing her in a Stetson, chaps, and diamond spurs. Cindy Ellen goes to the rodeo and wins the heart of the rancher's son, Joe Prince. As the clock strikes midnight Cindy Ellen runs toward her home, but drops one of her diamond spurs. Includes a note about the history of rodeos.

52   LUM, DARRELL H. Y.   *The Golden Slipper: A Vietnamese Legend.*
Ill. by Makiko Nagano. Troll, 1994
ISBN: 978-0-8167-3405-4
Country/Culture: Vietnam
Motifs: Clothing (shoes or boots)

Tam is kind and cares for animals. When it is time for the harvest festival, the animals repay her by finding the enchanted clothes she needs to attend. This version with the same illustrations and slightly different text has also been published by Troll under the title *Tam's Slipper* (entry 66).

53   MARCEAU-CHENKIE, BRITTANY.   *Naya: The Inuit Cinderella.*
Ill. by Shelley Brookes. Raven Rock Pub., 1999
ISBN: 978-1-894303-05-7
Country/Culture: Native American (Inuit)
Motifs: Clothing

Naya, a contemporary girl, lives a traditional Inuit life. She tries to make an amauti to wear to the Community Feast, but is too busy to finish it. On the night of the feast, she puts on the amauti and goes outside. The Northern Lights finish her dress and provide her with a dog sled team and golden sled to ride. Leaving the feast quickly, she drops a scrap of her own original beadwork that is used to find her.

54   MARTIN, CLAIRE.   *Boots and the Glass Mountain.*
Ill. by Gennady Spirin. Dial Books, 1992
ISBN: 978-0-8037-1110-5
Motifs: Gender role reversal
          Fruits and vegetables (apples)

A role-reversal tale where the protagonist is a scrawny boy, and the king is looking for a mate for the princess. She is placed at the top of a glass mountain and promised to whichever knight can ride his stallion to the top and collect three golden apples from the princess. The apples are used to identify Boots as the hero knight.

55 MARTIN, RAFE. *The Rough-Face Girl.*
Ill. by David Shannon. Putnam, 1992
ISBN: 978-0-399-21859-0
Country/Culture: Native American (Algonquin)
Motifs: Clothing

This girl's face is scarred because her sisters make her work too close to the fire. In the forest, the Invisible Being announces that he will marry the woman who can see him. The older sisters take everything their father has, and go to see him first. The rough-faced girl asks her father for new things, but he has nothing left but broken beads and worn-out moccasins. When the older girls get to the forest, the Invisible Being's sister asks what his bow is made of, but the girls can't answer. The rough-faced girl is able to answer the question correctly.

56 MARTIN, RAFE. *Twelve Months.*
Ill. by Vladyana Langer Krykorka. Stoddart Kids, 2000
ISBN: 978-0-7737-3249-0
Country/Culture: Slavic
Motifs: Seasons (autumn)
      Flowers
      Fruits and vegetables (apples)

Marushka lives with an aunt and cousin Holena. Out of jealousy, Holena and her mother decide to get rid of Marushka by sending her out in the middle of winter to find fruit and flowers. Each time, Marushka is able to bring back the items with the help of twelve mysterious men. Finally, her aunt and cousin get curious and go to the mountain. The men will not help them because the women are mean. The men disappear, and Holena and her mother get lost on the mountain.

57 MEDDAUGH, SUSAN. *Cinderella's Rat.*
Houghton Mifflin, 1997
ISBN: 978-0-395-86833-1
Motifs: Animals (mice or rats)

Told from the point of view of the rat who was turned into the coachman for Cinderella's carriage, this story focuses on the rat's experience of being changed into a person and the trouble he gets into when he acts on his rat instincts, such as helping himself to the cheese in the kitchen.

58   MEHTA, LILA.   *The Enchanted Anklet: A Cinderella Story from India.*

Ill. by Neela Chhaniara. Lilmur, 1985
ISBN: 978-0-9692729-0-8
Country/Culture: India
Motifs: Jewelry
            Animals (snakes)

Cinduri is the put-upon daughter in this version set in India. The magical character is a mysterious white snake with a red jewel on its head. The festival is Navaratri, and Cinduri loses a beautiful white gold and diamond anklet. It is found by a prince who is determined to find the owner. Includes a foreword, author's note, glossary, and pronunciation guide.

59   MINH, QUOC.   *Tam and Cam: The Ancient Vietnamese Cinderella Story.*

Ill. by Long Mai. East West Discovery Press, 2006
ISBN: 978-0-9701654-4-2
Country/Culture: Vietnam
Motifs: Fish
            Monsters, beasts, or magical creatures

Tam and Cam are stepsisters, and Cam is favored over Tam. Buddha appears to Tam and tells her to care for a magic fish. Cam and her mother find out about the fish and they kill and eat it out of spite. When Tam is chosen by the king as his wife, Cam and her mother kill her and put Cam in her place. Tam becomes a series of magical objects that the king loves, but that Cam destroys. When Tam morphs back into a human, the king finds her working in a shop and brings her back to the palace. In English and Vietnamese.

60   MINTERS, FRANCES.   *Cinder-Elly.*

Ill. by G. Brian Karas. Viking, 1994
ISBN: 978-0-670-84417-3
Motifs: Clothing (shoes or boots)
            Sports (basketball)

Set in contemporary Manhattan and told in rhyme. Instead of a ball, it is a basketball game that is the main event. The fairy godmother is Cinder-Elly's real-life godmother, and the ball gown is a satin shirt, red miniskirt, and glass high-top sneakers.

61   MITCHELL, MARIANNE. *Joe Cinders.*
Ill. by Bryan Langdo. Henry Holt, 2002
ISBN: 978-0-8050-6529-9
Country/Culture: Western
Motifs: Cowboys
          Clothing (shoes or boots)
          Gender role reversal

Joe Cinders is the put-upon brother at the ranch. On the night of the fiesta, he wanders into the range, where he meets a mysterious man wearing a serape and sombrero. The man gives Joe new fiesta clothes, including red boots, and turns Joe's horse into a bright red truck.

62   MYERS, BERNICE. *Sidney Rella and the Glass Sneaker.*
Atheneum, 1985
ISBN: 978-0-02-767790-4
Motifs: Clothing (shoes or boots)
          Sports (football)
          Gender role reversal

Sidney is a little boy who isn't old enough to play football with his big brothers. With a little help from a well-meaning but magically inexperienced fairy, he manages to win the big game in a pair of glass sneakers. It is the football coach who tries to find him when he disappears after the game.

63   NGUYEN, THI NHUAM. *Tam Cam: The Vietnamese Cinderella Story: A Bilingual Vietnamese Classic Tale.*
Ill. by Thi Hop Nguyen. The Gio'i, 1990
Country/Culture: Vietnam
Motifs: Clothing (shoes or boots)
          Fish
          Birds (crows)

Cam is Tam's stepsister. When they gather fish, Cam steals Tam's fish. Tam is told by a magic fish to feed the small fish every day. Cam and her mother catch and eat the magic fish out of jealousy. Tam buries the bones for ten days, and when she digs them up she finds a pair of shoes. A crow takes one to the Crown Prince. He marries Tam when he finds that the shoe is hers. In English and Vietnamese

64   NIMMO, JENNY. *The Starlight Cloak.*
Ill. by Justin Todd. Dial Books for Young Readers, 1993
ISBN: 978-0-8037-1508-0

Country/Culture: Ireland
Motifs: Stars

Oona is abused by her sisters and made a servant to them. Oona's foster grandmother comes to watch over her, and brings a small boy to help. With the help of some magic from the grandmother's starlight cloak, Oona wins the hand of the prince of Ermania. But one of Oona's sisters is not happy with that arrangement and schemes to make trouble for her sister.

65   OSMOND, ALAN, AND SUZANNE OSMOND.   *If the Shoe Fits.*
Ill. by Thomas Aarrestad. Ideals Children's Books, 1998
ISBN: 978-1-57102-133-5
Motifs: Sports (track and field)
           Gender role reversal
           Clothing (shoes or boots)

Prince James, the son of Cinderella and Prince Charming, competes in field day at school. The fairy godmother gives him magic track clothes, but his mean cousins steal them. James competes and does his best despite not having the clothes. The mean cousins wear the clothes, which turn back into a ballgown and slippers at noon on track day.

66   PALAZZO-CRAIG, JANET.   *Tam's Slipper: A Story from Vietnam.*
Ill. by Makiko Nagano. Troll, 1996
ISBN: 978-0-8167-4000-0
Country/Culture: Vietnam
Motifs: Clothing (shoes or boots)

Tam is kind to the animals that she cares for. In return, when it is time for the harvest festival they help her find the enchanted clothes and slippers she needs to attend. This version with the same illustrations and slightly different text has also been published by Troll under the title *The Golden Slipper* (entry 52).

67   PERKAL, STEPHANIE.   *Midnight: A Cinderella Alphabet.*
Ill. by Spencer Alston Bartsch. Shen's Books, 1997
ISBN: 978-1-885008-05-3
Motifs: Clothing (shoes or boots)

Each letter in the alphabet corresponds to a Cinderella story from around the world. China, Egypt, Germany, Portugal, India, Nigeria, Japan, France, Ireland, Korea, Vietnam, Norway, Russia, Philippines, Laos, and England are some of the countries represented. Includes source note.

68 PERLMAN, JANET. *Cinderella Penguin: Or, the Little Glass Flipper.*
Viking, 1992
ISBN: 978-0-670-84753-2
Motifs: Birds (penguins)
        Clothing (shoes or boots)

This version closely follows the original, with the exception that all the characters are penguins. The slipper that is left behind is actually a large glass flipper-shaped shoe. When the footmen come to try the shoe on the stepsisters, they drop it and it slides snuggly onto Cinderella's humongous webbed foot.

69 POLLOCK, PENNY. *The Turkey Girl: A Zuni Cinderella Story.*
Ill. by Ed Young. Little, Brown, 1995
ISBN: 978-0-316-71314-6
Country/Culture: Native American (Algonquin)
Motifs: Birds (turkeys)
        Jewelry

A young orphan herds the turkeys that belong to the wealthy families. When the herald-priest announces the Dance of the Sacred Bird, the turkey girl wishes to go. The turkeys speak to her, transform her clothes, and give her jewels. She must be back before nightfall, though, or the turkeys will leave. She goes to the dance and does not make it back before the sun sets. The turkeys have gone and that is why turkeys are now wild.

70 ROBERTS, LYNN. *Cinderella: An Art Deco Love Story.*
Ill. by David Roberts. Harry N. Abrams, 2001
ISBN: 978-0-8109-4168-7
Motifs: Clothing (shoes or boots)
        Music (jazz)

This Cinderella is originally named Greta and lives in a 1930s era city. She hears the announcement for a ball for Prince Roderick on the radio, but her evil stepsisters, Elvira and Ermintrude, leave her with no clothes to wear. A fairy appears and gives her beautiful clothes to wear and changes a rat, a leek, four mice, and two glowworms into her limousine and chauffeur. She attends the ball, dances with the prince, falls in love and, when he locates her the next day, marries him.

71   SAN SOUCI, ROBERT D.   *Cendrillon: A Caribbean Cinderella.*

Ill. by J. Brian Pinkney. Simon & Schuster, 1998
ISBN: 978-0-689-80668-1
Country/Culture: Caribbean
Motifs: Clothing (shoes or boots)

A washerwoman's mother leaves her a magic wand that will change one thing to another for a short time for someone you love. The washerwoman is Cendrillon's godmother. She uses her wand to make a carriage and gown so that Cendrillon can attend a party. Cendrillon leaves behind an embroidered slipper. Includes author's note and glossary of French Creole words and phrases.

72   SAN SOUCI, ROBERT D.   *Cinderella Skeleton.*

Ill. by David Catrow. Silver Whistle/Harcourt, 2000
ISBN: 978-0-15-202003-3
Motifs: Holidays (Halloween)
          Monsters, beasts, or magical creatures

Told in rhyming text. Cinderella Skeleton wants to go to Prince Charnel's Halloween Ball, and decides to take the initiative. She goes to the woods and summons up a good witch to get her what she needs to get there. When she must run away from the party, she leaves not a shoe, but her whole foot behind.

73   SAN SOUCI, ROBERT D.   *Little Gold Star: A Spanish American Cinderella Tale.*

Ill. by Sergio Martinez. Morrow Junior Books, 2000
ISBN: 978-0-688-14781-5
Country/Culture: Hispanic
Motifs: Stars
          Animals (sheep)

Teresa's father gives her a lamb, which her stepmother butchers. Cleaning the wool, Teresa meets a mysterious woman in blue who tells her to go care for a man and his child in a nearby hut. Teresa does and the woman returns and tells her that she is the Virgin Mary, the man was Joseph, and the baby was Jesus. Because of her kindness, Teresa receives a gold star on her forehead. After the fiesta, Teresa is located by the handsome Miguel. Teresa is given three tasks to complete, and again Mary intercedes.

74   SAN SOUCI, ROBERT D.   *Sootface: An Ojibwa Cinderella Story.*

Ill. by Daniel San Souci. Delacorte Press, 1994
ISBN: 978-0-385-31202-8
Country/Culture: Native American (Ojibwa)
Motifs: Clothing

Sootface is a young girl who is abused by her sisters. They smear her face with ashes and call her names. A mighty warrior who has the power to make himself invisible lets it be known that he will marry the woman who can see him, for that means that she is kind and honest. Sootface makes herself a new dress from birch bark and weeds, and although the whole village ridicules her, she goes to see him. After Sootface correctly identifies the warrior she is made beautiful by the warrior's sister, and he renames her Dawn-Light.

75   SCHROEDER, ALAN.   *Lily and the Wooden Bowl.*

Ill. by Yoriko Ito. Doubleday Books for Young Readers, 1994
ISBN: 978-0-385-30792-5
Country/Culture: Japan
Motifs: Birds (swans)

When Lily's grandmother dies, she leaves Lily three things — a paper swan, a rice paddle, and a bowl that she is to wear on her head to hide her beauty. The swan protects her from those who ridicule her, the rice paddle is used to make rice for a hundred people from a single grain, and when the wealthy farmer's son agrees to marry her despite the bowl on her head, it shatters, revealing her true beauty.

76   SCHROEDER, ALAN.   *Smoky Mountain Rose: An Appalachian Cinderella.*

Ill. by Brad Sneed. Dial Books for Young Readers, 1997
ISBN: 978-0-8037-1733-6
Country/Culture: Appalachia
Motifs: Clothing (shoes or boots)
       Dancing (square dance)

Told in mountain dialect. Rose lives in the hills of Appalachia. She doesn't get to go to the rich "feller's" square dance until a magic hog gets her the dress and glass shoes she needs. After she flees the dance, Seb goes looking for her and finds her out by the hog pen. Includes author's note.

77   SHORTO, RUSSELL. ***Cinderella's Stepsister.***
Ill. by T. Lewis. Carol Pub. Group, 1990
ISBN: 978-1-55972-054-0
Motifs: Clothing (shoes or boots)
A double-sided book. One side has the original story, the other has the story from one stepsister's point of view. The stepsister says they are actually nice people, but Cinderella is always telling stories. When she goes to the ball she dances with a man all night. She tells him she is a princess and he tells her about being a prince, though neither are. What they have in common is that they both tell stories. They get married and become storytellers.

78   SIERRA, JUDY. ***The Gift of the Crocodile: A Cinderella Story.***
Ill. by Reynold Ruffins. Simon & Schuster, 2000
ISBN: 978-0-689-82188-2
Country/Culture: Indonesia
Motifs: Clothing (shoes or boots)
       Animals (alligators or crocodiles)
In this tale set in Indonesia, the wish-granter is a crocodile, and the clothing she gives to Damura is a golden sarong and slippers. The plot takes an unusual twist when the stepmother and stepsisters kill Damura after she marries the prince. Damura appears to them as a ghost and they flee the palace and she is returned to life. Includes folklore note.

79   SILVERMAN, ERICA. ***Raisel's Riddle.***
Ill. by Susan Gaber. Farrar, Straus and Giroux, 1999
ISBN: 978-0-374-36168-6
Country/Culture: Jewish
Motifs: Holidays (Purim)
Raisel is a Jewish girl who works as a kitchen maid in the rabbi's house. When she is kind to a hungry woman, the woman grants Raisel three wishes, which she uses to attend the Purim celebration. There she meets the rabbi's son and asks him to answer a riddle. When she has to flee the party, it is the riddle that the son uses to find her again.

80   STEPTOE, JOHN. ***Mufaro's Beautiful Daughters: An African Tale.***
Lothrop, Lee & Shepard, 1987
ISBN: 978-0-688-04046-8
Country/Culture: Africa

Motifs: Animals (snakes)

Manyara is always in a bad temper and Nyasha is always kind. Nyasha finds a snake in her garden and sets him free. When the king announces that he is looking for a wife, Manyara wants to meet him first and leaves early. She is unkind to all she meets in the forest. Nyasha is good to them. When she gets to the palace she finds that the king was all of the creatures that they both met, and Manyara is sent screaming back home. Includes author's note.

81   TAKAYAMA, SANDI.   *Sumorella: A Hawai'i Cinderella Story.*
Ill. by Esther Szegedy. Bess Press, 1997
ISBN: 978-1-57306-027-1
Country/Culture: Hawaii
Motifs: Sports (wrestling)
          Gender role reversal

Mango Boy is the scrawny younger brother of two sumo wrestlers. When time comes for the big exhibition, Mango Boy can't go because he is too small. A passing peddler helps him out by using a spell to transform Mango Boy into Sumorella. When he has to flee at the end of the exhibition, Sumorella leaves behind his mawashi, or sumo loincloth, which is too small to fit any of the other sumos. Includes glossary of Hawaiian words.

82   THALER, MIKE.   *Cinderella Bigfoot.*
Ill. by Jared Lee. Scholastic, 1997
ISBN: 978-0-590-89826-3
Motifs: Clothing (shoes or boots)
          Animals (cows)
          Transportation (buses)

This version is littered with bad puns and wordplay. Cinderella's feet are so big that she doesn't get invited to the ball because she is considered a safety hazard. Her dairy godmother (a winged cow) insists that she attend, but makes her take a bus (it's cheaper). When she loses her size 87 AAA glass sneaker at the ball, the prince hires a "toe" truck to haul it around the kingdom. Part of the Happily Ever Laughter series.

83   THOMAS, JOYCE CAROL.   *The Gospel Cinderella.*
Ill. by David Diaz. Amistad, 2000
ISBN: 978-0-06-025387-5
Country/Culture: Louisiana

Motifs: Music (gospel)

Queen Mother Rhythm loses her baby during a hurricane. Crooked Foster Mother finds the baby and names her Cinderella. Cinderella grows up serving Crooked Foster Mother and her twin daughters. When Queen Mother Rhythm decides to retire from the Great Gospel Choir, the Prince of Music announces there will be auditions at the Great Gospel Convention. After singing at the audition, Cinderella becomes the new leader of the Great Gospel Choir and finds her real mother.

84   TING, RENEE.   *The Prince's Diary.*
      Ill. by Elizabeth O. Dulemba. Shen's Books, 2004
      ISBN: 978-1-885008-27-5
      Motifs: Clothing (shoes or boots)

Told in diary form from the prince's point of view. He recounts the many trials and tribulations of meeting various princesses, all while trying to find the beautiful girl he saw in the forest one day and nicknamed "Cinderella."

85   TRUSSELL-CULLEN, ALAN.   *The Real Cinderella Rap.*
      Ill. by Philip Webb. SRA School Group, 1994
      ISBN: 978-0-383-03771-8
      Motifs: Music (rap or hip-hop)

Cinderella is a real princess, but she doesn't have the good looks and snotty attitude of a princess. She is tall with big feet, spiked hair, and a loud voice. To find her a husband, her parents have a ball for all the princes, but no one will dance with her. So Cinderella plays drums with the band and tours with them. They get a record deal, become famous, and she meets a man who knows her beauty is on the inside.

86   WADE, MARGARET.   *Mei Ping and the Silver Shoes: A Chinese Cinderella Story.*
      Ill. by Leo Chen. McGraw-Hill School Division, 2002
      ISBN: 978-0-02-185100-3
      Country/Culture: China
      Motifs: Clothing (shoes or boots)

A magic ring of feathers grants Mei Ping her wishes. Instead of trying on the missing silver slipper to prove her identity, Mei Ping instead tries to steal the shoe back from the prince to return it to the magic feathers. She is caught in the act and recognized. Reading class edition from McGraw-Hill. Includes story questions and an activity at the back.

87   WHIPPLE, LAURA.   *If the Shoe Fits: Voices from Cinderella.*
Ill. by Laura Beingessner. Margaret K. McElderry Books, 2002
ISBN: 978-0-689-84070-8
Motifs: Clothing (shoes or boots)

This version stays close to the original, but is told in poems from multiple points of view. Each character provides a first-person account of his or her part of the story. The father's ghost regrets his decision to marry the stepmother, a cat mourns the loss of master and mistress, and the fairy godmother makes a mental list of things she needs to change so that Cinderella can go to the ball.

88   WILLARD, NANCY.   *Cinderella's Dress.*
Ill. by Jane Dyer. Blue Sky Press, 2003
ISBN: 978-0-590-56927-9
Motifs: Clothing (shoes or boots)
         Birds (magpies)

Two magpies "adopt" Cinderella and watch over her. When she doesn't have anything to wear to the ball, they make her a dress from the sparkling things they have stored in their nest. The stepsisters destroy the dress, but the magpies find that the one thing that they still have left in their nest is a gold ring that summons Cinderella's fairy godmother.

89   WILSON, BARBARA.   *Wishbones: A Folk Tale from China.*
Ill. by Meilo So. Bradbury Press, 1993
ISBN: 978-0-02-793125-9
Country/Culture: China
Motifs: Fish
         Clothing (shoes or boots)

Abused stepdaughter Yeh Hsien raises a beautiful red fish as a friend. Her stepmother is jealous and kills the fish and serves it for dinner. The bones prove to be magic, however, and grant Yeh Hsien whatever she wishes, including elegant clothing and shoes to go to the cave festival. On the way home she loses a slipper, which is found by the king, who makes her his wife.

THE COUNTRY MOUSE AND THE CITY MOUSE

As published in *Æsop's Fables: A New Revised Version from Original Sources...* (Frank F. Lovell & Company, 1884).

A COUNTRY MOUSE INVITED A TOWN MOUSE, an intimate friend, to pay him a visit, and partake of his country fare. As they were on the bare plough-lands, eating their wheat-stalks and roots pulled up from the hedge-row, the Town Mouse said to his friend: "You live here the life of the ants, while in my house is the horn of plenty. I am surrounded with every luxury, and if you will come with me, as I much wish you would, you shall have an ample share of my dainties." The Country Mouse was easily persuaded, and returned to town with his friend. On his arrival, the Town Mouse placed before him bread, barley, beans, dried figs, honey, raisins, and, last of all, brought a dainty piece of cheese from a basket. The Country Mouse, being much delighted at the sight of such good cheer, expressed his satisfaction in warm terms, and lamented his own hard fate. Just as they were beginning to eat, some one opened the door, and they both ran off squeaking, as fast as they could, to a hole so narrow that two could only find room in it by squeezing. They had scarcely again begun their repast when some one else entered to take something out of a cupboard, on which the two Mice, more frightened than before, ran away and hid themselves. At last the Country Mouse, almost famished, thus addressed his friend: "Although you have prepared for me so dainty a feast, I must leave you to enjoy it by yourself. It is surrounded by too many dangers to please me."

Better a little in safety, than an abundance surrounded by danger.

90 CRUMMEL, SUSAN STEVENS. *City Dog, Country Dog: Adapted from an Aesop Fable.*
Ill. by Dorothy Donohue. Marshall Cavendish, 2004
ISBN: 978-0-7614-5156-3
Country/Culture: France
Motifs: Animals (dogs)

A canine version of the story, set in France. The text makes extensive dog-related puns and places both dogs as artists who learn to appreciate each other's different lifestyles and still remain friends. Includes English translations of French phrases used and an author's note on French art and artists.

91 DAHLIE, ELIZABETH. *Bernelly and Harriet: The Country Mouse and the City Mouse.*
Little, Brown, 2002
ISBN: 978-0-316-60811-4
Motifs: Animals (mice or rats)
Clothing (shoes or boots)

An updated retelling of the story. Bernelly the country mouse teaches fly fishing during the summer and ties flies in the winter. She loves the country but wishes there was a shoe shop. City mouse Harriet is an artist during the winter and travels to exotic places during the summer. They have fun visiting each other, but decide that they are both in the right place in their own home.

92 HENRIETTA. *A Country Mouse in the Town House.*
Dorling Kindersley, 1995
ISBN: 978-0-7894-0021-5
Motifs: Animals (mice or rats)

A large-format read-aloud book illustrated with photographs. The story is told in rhyme and stays much the same as the original. One notable difference is when both mice flee from the maid in the city for the country. In this version both mice remain in the country rather than one returning to the city.

93   SUMMERS, KATE.   *Milly and Tilly: The Story of a Town Mouse and a Country Mouse.*
Ill. by Maggie Kneen. Dutton Children's Books, 1997
ISBN: 978-0-525-45801-2
Motifs: Animals (mice or rats)

This version stays close to the original fable. Tilly lives in the country and loves country life. Milly comes to visit from the city but feels the country is much too quiet. Tilly visits the city and is impressed with all the things that Milly owns and delicacies that she eats, but finds living with a cat too stressful.

THE EMPEROR'S NEW CLOTHES

Abridged from *Stories from Hans Andersen* (Hodder & Stoughton, 1911)

ONCE THERE WAS AN EMPEROR WHO WAS SO FOND OF clothes that he spent all his money on them. He did not care about his soldiers, or the theatre, or for riding, but he had a costume for every hour in the day.

One day two swindlers came to town. They pretended to be weavers and said they knew how to weave the most beautiful cloth imaginable. Not only was the cloth unusually fine, but the clothes that were made of it had the ability to become invisible to every person who was a fool.

"By wearing these clothes," thought the Emperor, "I will be able to discover who in my kingdom is a fool. I must order some."

So he paid the two swindlers to begin at once.

The pair put up looms and pretended to weave. They asked for silk and thread, which they put into their own bags, and they worked away at empty looms.

"I should like to know how the weavers are doing," thought the Emperor, but he would send somebody else first.

"I will send my minister," thought the Emperor. "He is clever! He will be able to see the cloth."

So the minister went to the swindlers.

"Heaven preserve us!" thought the minister, "I can't see it!" But he did not say so.

Both the swindlers asked him to come look closely. They pointed to the empty loom, and the poor old minister stared, but he could not see anything.

"Good heavens!" he thought. "Am I a fool? I cannot say I see nothing."

So the minister said, "Oh, it is beautiful! I will tell the Emperor how wonderful it is."

"We are delighted," said the swindlers, and they asked for more money, more silk, and more thread, which they put into their own pockets.

Soon the Emperor sent another official to see the cloth. The same thing happened to him as to the minister; he could see nothing at all.

"Is it not beautiful?" said both the swindlers, pretending to show the fabric.

"I am not a fool!" thought the man, so he praised what he did not see.

"It is absolutely charming!" he told the Emperor.

Now the Emperor wanted to see the cloth. So he went to visit the impostors with his courtiers.

"It is magnificent!" the courtiers said. "See, your Majesty, what a design! What colors!" For each believed the other could see it.

"What!" thought the Emperor. "I see nothing at all! Am I a fool? Why, nothing could be worse!"

"Oh, it is beautiful!" agreed the Emperor, and he nodded his satisfaction at the empty loom.

Everyone looked, but none would say they saw nothing. They all exclaimed, "It is very beautiful!" and advised the Emperor to wear a suit made of this cloth in a parade the next day.

The swindlers sat up that whole night, pretending to get the Emperor's new clothes ready. They pretended to take the cloth off the loom. They cut in the air with a pair of scissors, and they stitched with threadless needles. At last they said they were ready.

The Emperor entered the room, and both rogues raised an arm as if they were holding something. They said: "See how beautiful it is? It is so light one might think he had nothing on!"

"Will your imperial majesty please take off your clothes," said the impostors, "so that we can dress you?"

The Emperor took off his clothes, and the impostors pretended to dress him. The Emperor turned and looked in the mirror.

"Well, I am ready," said the Emperor. "Aren't these wonderful?" And then he turned around again, pretending to look at his grand clothes.

"How beautiful his majesty looks! How becoming they are!" cried all the courtiers.

"Your canopy is outside," said the master of the ceremonies.

The chamberlains who were to carry the train stooped and pretended to lift it with both hands. They dared not let it appear that they could not see it.

The Emperor walked under the canopy, and everybody exclaimed, "How beautiful his clothes are! They fit to perfection!" No one would admit they could not see the clothes.

"He has nothing on," said a little child.

"Oh, listen to the innocent," said his father. "The child says he has nothing on!" But one person whispered this to another.

At last all the people cried "He has nothing on! He has nothing on!"

And the Emperor knew it was true, but he thought "the procession must continue," so held himself higher than ever, and went on.

✦

94   CALMENSON, STEPHANIE. *The Principal's New Clothes.*
Ill. by Denise Brunkus. Scholastic, 1989
ISBN: 978-0-590-41822-5
Motifs: Clothing
         School

The principal, Mr. Bundy, is a vain and snappy dresser. The tricksters Moe and Ivy show up at the school and promise to make him a suit that can only be seen by those who are smart and good at their job. It is at the school assembly that a kindergartener finally tells the truth.

95   DELUISE, DOM. *King Bob's New Clothes.*
Ill. by Christopher Santoro. Simon & Schuster, 1996
ISBN: 978-0-671-89727-7
Motifs: Clothing

This version is told as a comedian's monologue with personal comments and questions directed to the audience. In the end, King Bob puts the tailors who duped him to work making clothes for the poor, and he apologizes to his people for being so vain. Includes recipes for "royal" dishes: Chicken a la King, King in a Blanket, King Crab Cakes, and King Crown Cake.

96   DEMI. *The Emperor's New Clothes: A Tale Set in China.*
Margaret K. McElderry Books, 2000
ISBN: 978-0-689-83068-6
Country/Culture: China
Motifs: Clothing

A provincial Chinese emperor takes much pride in dressing in the finest clothes. Two strangers appear in the province and promise the emperor that they can make him magical clothes that only clever people can see. Not wanting to be considered a fool, the emperor has them make the clothes even though he can't see them. Only a small child has the innocence to point out that the emperor is naked. Includes an author's note on the illustrations.

97   GILL, VINCE. *The Emperor's New Clothes.*
Ill. by Carol Newsom. Dutton Children's Books, 2003
ISBN: 978-0-525-47152-3

Motifs: Music (country)
        Clothing

This version is retold by the singer as a country music story in a contemporary setting. The "emperor" is an important businessman who is vain about his clothes. He decides to make all of his clothes western wear, and hires two swindlers to make his wardrobe. They tell him they will make him belt buckles of gold, hand-tailored jackets studded with rhinestones, and blue jeans stitched with silver thread, all of which only very clever people can see. Includes a CD of the story and songs.

98   GOODE, DIANE. *Dinosaur's New Clothes.*
Blue Sky Press, 1999
ISBN: 978-0-590-38360-8
Motifs: Dinosaurs
        Clothing

Tyrannosaurus Rex, the dinosaur king, loves to dress in the finest clothes. One day, two swindlers appear and promise the king that they can make him magic clothes that only smart people can see. Not wanting to be considered stupid, the king has them make the clothes. All his ministers and subjects tell him how beautiful the clothes are. Only a small child has the temerity to point out that the king is in his underwear. Includes author's note on dinosaurs.

99   LASKY, KATHRYN. *The Emperor's Old Clothes.*
Ill. by David Catrow. Harcourt Brace, 1999
ISBN: 978-0-15-200384-5
Motifs: Clothing
        Animals
        Farms

Henry is a simple farmer who is content as he is. When he finds the emperor's discarded old clothes, Henry puts them on and fancies himself a grand gentleman. His farm animals tease and laugh at him for acting so pretentious. Finally, he comes to his senses and sees that he is best at being himself.

100   PERLMAN, JANET. *The Emperor Penguin's New Clothes.*
Viking, 1995
ISBN: 978-0-670-85864-4
Motifs: Birds (penguins)
        Clothing

A king, who is an emperor penguin, loves to dress in the richest clothes. Two tailors come to his kingdom and make the king clothes from magic cloth that only clever people can see. Only a small child has the innocence to point out that the emperor is naked when he wears them.

101 YOLEN, JANE. *King Long Shanks.*
Ill. by Victoria Chess. Harcourt Brace, 1998
ISBN: 978-0-15-200013-4
Motifs: Animals (frogs or toads)
        Clothing

This stays close to the original version, but all the characters are frogs. The Frog King is vain about how long and green his legs are. In order to show them off, he contracts with two scoundrels to make him a wardrobe that only beautiful and wise frogs can see.

GOLDILOCKS

Abridged from *English Fairy Tales Collected by Joseph Jacobs* (Third edition, revised. G.P. Putnam's Sons, 1902)

THE STORY OF THE THREE BEARS

ONCE UPON A TIME THERE WERE THREE BEARS, who lived together in a house in the woods. One of them was a Little, Small, Wee Bear; and one was a Middle-sized Bear, and the other was a Great, Huge Bear. They had each a pot for their porridge, a chair to sit in, and a bed to sleep in.

One day, after they had made the porridge for their breakfast, and poured it into their porridge-pots, they walked out into the wood while the porridge was cooling. While they were walking, a little old Woman came to the house. The door was not fastened, so the little old Woman opened the door, and went in; and well pleased she was when she saw the porridge on the table, and set about helping herself.

So first she tasted the porridge of the Great, Huge Bear, and that was too hot, and then she tasted the porridge of the Middle Bear, and that was too cold, then she went to the porridge of the Little, Small, Wee Bear, and tasted that; and it was just right. So she ate it all up.

Then the little old Woman sat down in the chair of the Great, Huge Bear, and that was too hard. Then she sat down in the chair of the Middle Bear, and that was too soft. Then she sat down in the chair of the Little, Small, Wee Bear, and that just right. So she seated herself in it, and there she sat till the bottom of the chair came out.

Then the little old Woman went upstairs into the chamber where the three Bears slept. First she lay down upon the bed of the Great, Huge Bear; but that was too high at the head. Next she lay down upon the bed of the Middle Bear; and that was too high at the foot. Then she lay down upon the bed of the Little, Small, Wee Bear; and that was just right. So she lay there till she fell asleep.

By this time the Three Bears thought their porridge would be cool enough; so they came home to breakfast. The little old Woman had left the spoon of the Great, Huge Bear, standing in his porridge.

"Somebody has been at my porridge!" said the Great, Huge Bear, in his great, rough, gruff voice.

And when the Middle Bear looked at his, he saw that the spoon was standing in it too.

"Somebody has been at my porridge!" said the Middle Bear in his middle voice.

Then the Little, Small, Wee Bear looked at his, and there was the spoon in the porridge-pot, but the porridge was all gone.

"Somebody has been at my porridge, and has eaten it all up!" said the Little, Small, Wee Bear, in his little, small, wee voice.

Upon this the Three Bears, seeing that some one had entered their house, began to look about them. The little old Woman had not put the cushion straight when she rose from the chair of the Great, Huge Bear.

"Somebody has been sitting in my chair!" said the Great, Huge Bear, in his great, rough, gruff voice.

And the little old Woman had squatted down the soft cushion of the Middle Bear.

"Somebody has been sitting in my chair!" said the Middle Bear, in his middle voice.

And you know what the little old Woman had done to the third chair.

"Somebody has been sitting in my chair and has sat the bottom out of it!" said the Little, Small, Wee Bear, in his little, small, wee voice.

Then the Three Bears thought it necessary that they should make further search; so they went upstairs. The little old Woman had pulled the pillow of the Great, Huge Bear out of its place.

"Somebody has been lying in my bed!" said the Great, Huge Bear, in his great, rough, gruff voice.

And the little old Woman had pulled the bolster of the Middle Bear out of its place.

"Somebody has been lying in my bed!" said the Middle Bear, in his middle voice.

And when the Little, Small, Wee Bear came to look at his bed, there was the little old Woman's ugly, dirty head.

"Somebody has been lying in my bed,—and here she is!" said the Little, Small, Wee Bear, in his little, small, wee voice.

When the little old Woman had heard the little, small, wee voice of the Little, Small, Wee Bear, it was so sharp, and so shrill, that it awakened her at once. When she saw the Three Bears she tumbled herself out of the bed and jumped out an open window, and the Three Bears never saw her again.

102   BAILEY, LINDA.   ***Gordon Loggins and the Three Bears.***
Ill. by Tracy Walker. Kids Can Press, 1997
ISBN: 978-1-55074-362-3
Motifs: Animals (bears)
       Food (breads or grains)

On a trip to the library, Gordon gets lost in a book and visits a mysterious forest and meets the three bears. The bears have a story to perform, and though Gordon isn't Goldilocks, they have him stand in for her. Unfortunately, Gordon doesn't always do exactly what he is supposed to do, and he fractures the story himself.

103   BRETT, JAN.   ***The Three Snow Bears.***
Putnam, 2007
ISBN: 978-0-399-24792-7
Country/Culture: Native American (Inuit)
Motifs: Animals (bears)
       Animals (dogs)
       Seasons (winter)
       Food (soup or stew)

Three polar bears go for a walk while the soup cools in their igloo. While they are gone, a young Inuit girl who has lost her dog team goes into their home and tastes the soup, tries on their boots, and falls asleep in their bed. When she is awakened, she runs outside to find that the bears have brought her sled team back for her.

104   BUEHNER, CARALYN.   ***Goldilocks and the Three Bears.***
Ill. by Mark Buehner. Dial Books for Young Readers, 2007
ISBN: 978-0-8037-2939-1
Motifs: Animals (bears)

This version stays close to the original story. The characters have been updated and Goldilocks skips rope throughout the story. When the bears return from their walk, they find the mess Goldilocks has made and are convinced that a monster or an alien has entered their home.

105   CATALANO, DOMINIC.   ***Santa and the Three Bears.***
Boyds Mills Press, 2000
ISBN: 978-1-56397-864-7
Motifs: Holidays (Christmas)
       Animals (bears)

When Santa goes to deliver the presents Christmas Eve, Mrs. Claus and the elves arrange a surprise party for him. It is the three bears who come in from the cold and take advantage of the party preparations. Working together, they make everything right again just before Santa returns.

106   COLLINS, SHEILA HÉBERT. *Jolie Blonde and the Three Heberts: A Cajun Twist to an Old Tale.*
Ill. by Patrick Soper. Pelican, 1999
ISBN: 978-1-56554-324-9
Country/Culture: Cajun
Motifs: Animals (bears)
          Food (soup or stew)

The story is similar to the original, but set in Cajun country. The three bears are a human family with the surname Hébert, who go for a boat ride in the swamp while they wait for the gumbo to cool. Jolie Blonde is a girl from Thibidoux who is wandering around the bayou when she sees the empty house and lets herself in. Includes definitions and pronunciation guide for French Cajun words on each page, and a recipe for Mama Hébert's Gumbo.

107   CRUMP, FRED H. *Afrotina and the Three Bears.*
Winston-Derek Publishers, 1991
ISBN: 978-1-55523-195-8
Country/Culture: African American
Motifs: Animals (bears)
          Clothing
          Food (breads or grains)

Afrotina goes walking in the woods to show off her new clothes. When she comes to the bears' cave, she invites herself in. The bears come home and find her and they scold her for her poor manners. She apologizes and makes everything right again, including giving Baby Bear her own dinner from home.

108   DELUISE, DOM. *Goldilocks.*
Ill. by Christopher Santoro. Simon & Schuster, 1992
ISBN: 978-0-671-74690-2
Motifs: Animals (bears)
          Food (breads or grains)

This version is told as a comedian's monologue with first-person comments and questions directed to the reader. Goldilocks is supposed to be doing her homework when she goes for a walk and finds the bears' house. Even though she messes up the house and creates complete chaos, the bears are polite enough to ask Goldilocks to stay for lunch. She accepts the invitation, apologizes for the intrusion, and becomes good friends with the bear family.

109   DENIM, SUE. *The Dumb Bunnies.*
Ill. by Dav Pilkey. Blue Sky Press, 1994
ISBN: 978-0-590-47708-6
Motifs: Animals (rabbits or hares)
Food (breads or grains)

There are three dumb bunnies: Momma Bunny, who is really dumb; Poppa Bunny, who is even dumber; and Baby Bunny, who is the dumbest of them all. Little Red Goldilocks visits their house while they are out and sleeps in the porridge, eats the beds, and uses Baby Bunny's pimple cream.

110   DUVAL, KATHY. *The Three Bears' Halloween.*
Ill. by Paul Meisel. Holiday House, 2007
ISBN: 978-0-8234-2032-2
Motifs: Holidays (Halloween)
Animals (bears)

The three bears go out trick-or-treating on Halloween. One of the houses they visit is occupied by a witch who happens to have very familiar gold hair. She scares them into running into the house where they eat her food, and plays tricks on them that make them mess up her furniture and hide in the beds.

111   ERNST, LISA CAMPBELL. *Goldilocks Returns.*
Simon & Schuster, 2000
ISBN: 978-0-689-82537-8
Motifs: Animals (bears)
Food (breads or grains)

Flash forward fifty years and Goldilocks feels guilty for the rude way she behaved at the bears' house. She goes back to the house and tries to make things right again, only to botch that visit as well. She changes the locks, decorates the house, and exchanges the food for healthier choices.

112   FEARNLEY, JAN. *Mr. Wolf and the Three Bears.*
Harcourt, 2002
ISBN: 978-0-15-216423-2
Motifs: Animals (bears)
Animals (wolves or coyotes)
Cooking

Mr. Wolf and his grandma go to great lengths to make a nice birthday party for Baby Bear, but Goldilocks shows up and ruins everything. When Grandma Wolf remembers the special ingredient to her Golden Pie, everybody except Goldilocks lives happily ever after. Includes recipes for Baby Bear's Birthday Cake, Mommy Bear's Sandwiches, Daddy Bear's Huff Puffs, Cheesy Snipsnap Biscuits, and Grandma's Golden Pie.

113   GRANOWSKY, ALVIN.   *Bears Should Share!*

Ill. by Annie Lunsford. Steck-Vaughn, 1995

ISBN: 978-0-8114-7127-5

Motifs: Animals (bears)

Food (breads or grains)

Part of the publisher's Point of View series. This edition has the original tale told in the first part, and then the book is turned over to read Goldilocks's side of the story. In the version narrated by Goldilocks, Baby Bear invites her to the house and to their food, chairs, and beds because "bears should share!"

114   KURTZ, JOHN.   *Goldilocks and the Three Bears.*

Jump at the Sun/Hyperion Books for Children, 2004

ISBN: 978-0-7868-0952-3

Country/Culture: African American

Motifs: Animals (bears)

Food (breads or grains)

In this standard retelling of the original story, the characters are portrayed as African Americans. In this version, Goldilocks is held responsible for all the mess she made and instead of running away she stays and fixes everything. Part of the Jump at the Sun Fairy-tale Classics series.

115   LAIRD, DONIVEE MARTIN.   *Wili Wai Kula and the Three Mongooses.*

Ill. by Carol Jossem. Barnaby Books, 1983

ISBN: 978-0-940350-04-5

Country/Culture: Hawaii

Motifs: Animals (mongooses)

An account of the original story set in Hawaii. The three Mongooses take a walk while their rice and Portuguese sausage cools. The chairs are made from koa wood, and the beds are pūne'e—low, flat couches with no arms. Includes a glossary of Hawaiian words and pidgin dialect used and a pronunciation guide.

116   LESTER, HELEN.   *Tackylocks and the Three Bears.*
Ill. by Lynn Munsinger. Houghton Mifflin, 2002
ISBN: 978-0-618-22490-6
Motifs: Birds (penguins)

Tacky the Penguin stars as Goldilocks in a play for Mrs. Beakly's first-grade class. When the play starts to get confused, the younger penguins, who were bored with the performance at first, find that Tacky's boisterous personality and madcap antics change the story into lively entertainment.

117   LOWELL, SUSAN.   *Dusty Locks and the Three Bears.*
Ill. by Randy Cecil. Henry Holt, 2001
ISBN: 978-0-8050-5862-8
Country/Culture: Western
Motifs: Animals (bears)
          Food (breads or grains)

Dusty Locks is dirty, ornery, and ill-behaved. When she visits the bears' house, it isn't the mess she makes as much as the smell she leaves behind that tells the bears where she is. When she flees the house, she runs straight back home where her mother washes, scrubs, and combs her into a whole new girl.

118   MACDONALD, ALAN.   *Beware of the Bears!*
Ill. by Gwyneth Williamson. Little Tiger Press, 1998
ISBN: 978-1-888444-28-5
Motifs: Animals (bears)
          Animals (wolves or coyotes)

Seeing the mess that Goldilocks made in their house, the three bears go to her house and make an even bigger mess. Everything changes when they discover that it's not her house, but the house of another fairy tale character, Big Bad Wolf.

119   MEYERS, ANNE.   *Goldilocks Comes Back.*
Ill. by Roberta Collier-Morales. Steck-Vaughn, 1997
ISBN: 978-0-8172-6422-2
Motifs: Animals (bears)
          Food (breads or grains)

After having experienced Goldilocks's antics the first time, Baby Bear creates some well-placed booby traps to make certain that the next time she visits everything will not be so cozy for her. With the help of Little Pig, he puts glue on the porridge spoon, ties pots and pans to the rocking chair, and puts a frog in Baby Bear's bed.

128   TURKLE, BRINTON. *Deep in the Forest.*
Dutton, 1976
ISBN: 978-0-525-28617-2
Motifs: Animals (bears)
A wordless book. It is a standard retelling, but the roles have been reversed. In this version, the home invader is a bear cub and the owners are humans. The cub enters a cabin while the family is out and eats the food, breaks the chairs, and tears up the bedding. When the family returns and finds the mess they use a broom to shoo the cub out of the house.

129   UMANSKY, KAYE. *A Chair for Baby Bear.*
Ill. by Chris Fisher. Barron's Educational Series, 2004
ISBN: 978-0-7641-5789-9
Motifs: Animals (bears)
Mama and Papa Bear take Baby Bear to the chair store so he can pick out one to replace the chair that Goldilocks broke. On the way there he imagines all the different types of chairs he might select, but when he gets there none of them are "just right." Returning home, he finds that Goldilocks has replaced his old one, and that one is just perfect.

HANSEL AND GRETEL

Adapted from *Household Stories by the Brothers Grimm* (Macmillan and Company, 1886).

HANSEL AND GRETHEL

NEAR THE FOREST LIVED A WOODCUTTER AND HIS WIFE, and his two children, Hansel and Grethel. They were very poor and had little to eat. This worried the woodcutter and one night he said to his wife, "What will become of us? We cannot feed our children."

"In the morning," answered the wife, "we will take the children into the forest and leave them there. Then we shall be rid of them."

"No, wife," said the man, "I cannot do that to my children."

"You fool," said she, "then everyone will starve; you had better get the coffins ready." And so she badgered him until he consented.

But the children heard the talk. When the parents went to sleep Hansel comforted his little sister, and said, "Don't cry, Grethel, God will help us."

Early the next morning the wife gave each a little piece of bread and took them to the wood. On the way Hansel made crumbs from his bread and dropped them, thinking he and Grethel could follow the crumbs back home.

Deep in the wood, the wife told the children, "Sit there, we are going to cut wood. When we are finished we will fetch you."

But they did not come back for the children. When the moon rose the children got up, but they could not find the crumbs for the birds had eaten them. So they lay down under a tree and fell asleep.

In the morning they found in front of them a house built of bread, roofed with cakes, and with windows of sugar.

"This will make a fine meal," said Hansel. "Grethel, come and eat." So they began to eat.

Then a voice called inside,

"Nibble, nibble, like a mouse,

Who is nibbling at my house?"

And the children answered, "It is just the wind," and went on eating.

After a bit the door opened, and an aged woman appeared. Hansel and Grethel were frightened, but the woman said, "Ah, children, come inside and eat." She took each by the hand, led them inside, and filled them with good things to eat. When they were finished, they lay down and went to sleep.

But the old woman was a really a wicked witch who had made the candy house appear to them. When they were plump, she intended to make them into a child-pie.

When they awoke, the witch grabbed Hansel, dragged him to the stable, and shut him in a cage.

Then she went back to Grethel and told her, "Get up and cook for me. We need to fatten your brother. When he is fat enough I will eat him."

So Grethel cooked for her brother so that the witch could fatten him up. Each morning the old woman visited the cage and demanded, "Hansel, show me your finger, that I may see if you are fat enough."

But Hansel would hold out a chicken bone, and the old woman's weak eyes could not make out what it was. When four weeks had passed the witch lost patience and could wait no longer.

The witch said, "Now is the time, girl. Go check the oven, and I will make my pie."

But Grethel said, "I don't know how to do it. How do I start?"

"Stupid goose," said the old woman, "You put your head in like this, see?" And she stooped down and put her head in the oven's mouth. Then Grethel pushed her in, and closed the grate behind her. The witch screamed and screamed, until she was no more.

So Grethel went to free Hansel, and he flew out like a bird from its cage. They danced around happily, and hugged each other. When they settled, they looked about the house, and they found chests of pearls and precious stones in every corner.

"This is better than bread crumbs," said Hansel, as he filled his pockets and Grethel filled her apron.

And so they left that place, and went back to the wood. But this time the way grew more and more familiar, until they saw their father's house. Then they ran and rushed in the door, and fell on their father's neck. The man had not rested since he left his children in the wood; and now the wife was dead. When Grethel opened her apron the pearls and precious stones scattered all over the room, and Hansel took one handful after another out of his pocket, and all care was at an end, and they lived in great joy together.

130   BLACK, SHEILA.   *The Witch's Story.*
Ill. by Arlene Klemushin. Carol Pub. Group, 1991
ISBN: 978-1-55972-080-9
Motifs: Food (desserts)
      Animals (cats)
      Animals (mice or rats)
      Monsters, beasts, or magical creatures

A reverse-printed book with the original tale on one side and a version told by the witch on the other. According to the witch, the children were mean and bratty and tried to throw her into the oven when she hadn't done anything. To get them to behave she turns them into mice.

131   CRUMP, FRED H.   *Hakim and Grenita: Hansel and Gretel.*
Winston-Derek Publishers, 1991
ISBN: 978-1-55523-298-6
Country/Culture: African American
Motifs: Monsters, beasts, or magical creatures

This account stays close to the original tale with the addition of African American characters. When Grenita shoves the witch into the oven, all the witch's magic spells are broken and the children are set free. Along with the text, each illustration is accompanied by a banner describing the scene depicted.

132   DELUISE, DOM.   *Dom DeLuise's Hansel and Gretel.*
Ill. by Christopher Santoro. Simon & Schuster, 1997
ISBN: 978-0-689-81202-6
Motifs: Food (desserts)
      Fruits and vegetables

Told as a comedian's monologue with personal comments and questions directed to the audience. Hansel and Gretel flee from their stepmother who insists that they eat nothing but healthy food. In the woods, they find the house of Glut Annie Stout who holds them captive as kitchen help. They are forced to make pastries and other rich desserts until they finally escape to find healthy foods. Includes recipes for Golden Dreams fat-free chicken soup and sugarless apple pie.

133   GORDON, DAVID.   *Hansel and Diesel.*
HarperCollins, 2006
ISBN: 978-0-06-058122-0
Motifs: Transportation (trucks)
      Construction

Hansel and Diesel are young trucks who venture out of the house look-ing for fuel. What they find is a beautiful, brightly lit truck stop with col-ored lights and brand new tires in the middle of the junkyard. The Wicked Winch convinces them to sleep there, but tries to shred them for scrap metal as they sleep. They are rescued by their parents who went looking for them and found the trail of bolts that Hansel left.

134 HÉBERT-COLLINS, SHEILA. *'T Pousette et 't Poulette: A Cajun Hansel and Gretel.*
Ill. by Patrick Soper. Pelican, 2001
ISBN: 978-1-56554-764-3
Country/Culture: Cajun
Motifs: Food
       Monsters, beasts, or magical creatures

Left in the swamp by their stepmother, the twins find a cottage that is made of Cajun food: boudin (sausage), beignets (doughnuts), pralines, and fried crawfish tails. The witch lures them inside with the smell of jam-balaya and locks Hansel up in order to fatten him up for her sauce patate (potato stew). Gretel pushes the witch into the stew and frees her brother. They then discover a treasure in the cottage that once belonged to the pi-rate Jean Lafitte. Includes pronunciation guide and definitions for French words on each page. Includes a recipe for La Sauce Patate.

135 THALER, MIKE. *Hanzel and Pretzel.*
Ill. by Jared D. Lee. Scholastic, 1997
ISBN: 978-0-590-89827-0
Motifs: Food (desserts)
       Food (soup or stew)
       Monsters, beasts, or magical creatures

Hanzel and Pretzel venture into the Deep Dark Woods where their mother told them not to go. There they meet the Horrible Witch who keeps Hanzel captive to fatten up and eat, and makes Pretzel polish her caul-dron. She feeds Hanzel pieces of her house until the children are able to escape. Filled with puns and wordplay. Part of the Happily Ever Laugh-ter series.

JACK AND THE BEANSTALK

Abridged from *English Fairy Tales Collected by Joseph Jacobs* (3rd edition, revised. G.P. Putnam's Sons, 1902).

THERE WAS ONCE A POOR WIDOW, HER SON NAMED JACK, and a cow. All Jack and his mother had to live on was the milk the cow gave. But one morning she gave no milk.

"What shall we do?" worried the widow.

"Mother," said Jack. "I'll go to market and sell the cow, and then we'll have the money."

So he took the cow off to market. On the way he met an old man who asked, "Where are you off to?"

"I'm going to market to sell our cow," Jack replied.

"How about I swap you for these?" The man pulled some odd beans out of his pocket.

"I think not," said Jack.

"But these are magic beans," said the man. "They will grow a beanstalk up to the sky."

"Really?" Jack said.

"Really. If not, you can have your cow back."

"All right," said Jack, and traded him the cow for the beans.

Jack went back home, and his mother met him at the door.

"How much did you get for her?"

"I got these magic beans. They're magical, plant them over-night and——"

"What!" said Jack's mother. "You traded the best milker in the parish for beans?" And she threw the beans out the window and sent Jack to bed without supper.

The next morning, Jack jumped up and went to the window. And there was a beanstalk that went up and up till it reached the sky.

Jack opened his window and climbed up the beanstalk. He climbed and he climbed till at last he reached the clouds. In the clouds was a great big house, and on the doorstep there was a great big woman.

"Good morning, mum," said Jack, politely. "Could you give me some breakfast?"

The great big tall woman said, "You'll be breakfast if you're not careful. There's nothing my man likes better than broiled boys on toast."

"Please give me something to eat, mum," said Jack. "I may as well be broiled, as die of hunger."

Well, the ogre's wife wasn't such a bad sort, so she gave him some food. Thump! thump! thump! The house trembled with footsteps.

"It's my man," said the wife, "Quick, jump in here." And she hid Jack in the oven.

The giant sat down at the table. "Ah what's that I smell?

Fee-fi-fo-fum,

I smell the blood of an Englishman,

Be he alive, or be he dead

I'll grind his bones to make my bread."

"Nonsense, dear, that's just the boy from last night's dinner that you smell," said his wife.

So the giant ate his breakfast, and sat down to count his gold. Shortly he began snoring, and Jack made his escape. On his way out, Jack helped himself to one of the bags of gold, which he took back to his mother.

"See, mother," he said to her. "Those were magic beans."

They lived on that gold for some time, and when it was gone Jack decided to try his luck up the beanstalk once more. So he climbed up to the clouds again, and there was the great big woman.

"Good morning, mum," said Jack, as bold as brass. "Could you be so good as to give me something to eat?"

All happened as it did before. The giant came in, ate his breakfast, and then he said: "Wife, bring me my hen." And when she did, the ogre said: "Lay," and it laid an egg all of gold. After a bit, the giant fell asleep.

Then Jack crept out of his hiding spot, caught hold of the golden hen, and was back at his house, lickety-split.

It wasn't many weeks before Jack determined to have another go at the beanstalk. So he went again to the top. And all was as before, except that when the giant was finished eating, he said: "Bring me my golden harp." His wife brought it and the giant said: "Sing!" and the golden harp sang beautifully. And it did till the ogre fell asleep.

Then Jack came out of his hiding spot, grabbed the harp, and dashed to the door. But the harp called out: "Master! Master!" and the ogre woke up to see Jack running off.

Jack ran as fast as he could, and then climbed down and down till he was home. Then he called out: "Mother! Bring me an axe!" Jack grabbed the axe and chopped at the beanstalk. The beanstalk toppled over, and the ogre fell down and broke his crown. And Jack and his mother lived happily ever after.

136   BARWIN, GARY.   *The Magic Moustache.*
Ill. by Stephane Jorisch. New York, 1999
ISBN: 978-1-55037-607-4
Motifs: Gardening
Hair

A disembodied nose is given a magic mustache for a pair of glasses. His parents, both eyeballs, are disgusted with the trade and throw out the mustache. The mustache grows into a giant beard reaching to the sky, and the nose climbs up it to find a giant mouth waiting for him.

137   BIRDSEYE, TOM.   *Look Out, Jack! The Giant Is Back!*
Ill. by Will Hillenbrand. Holiday House, 2001
ISBN: 978-0-8234-1450-5
Motifs: Gardening
Monsters, beasts, or magical creatures

This version starts where the original story ends. After Jack steals the giant's gold, harp, and goose, he is pursued by the giant's brother and he and his mother flee to America. The giant soon finds them there, however, and Jack has to think up new ways to trick him into leaving them alone.

138   BRIGGS, RAYMOND.   *Jim and the Beanstalk.*
Coward-McCann, 1980
ISBN: 978-0-14-050077-6
Motifs: Gardening
Monsters, beasts, or magical creatures

In a contemporary city, Jim has no idea why a beanstalk mysteriously grows outside his window. Climbing it, he befriends a giant who has low self-esteem. When they become acquainted, Jim gets the giant the teeth, glasses, and wig he needs to make him feel better about himself.

139   CRUMP, FRED H.   *Jamako and the Beanstalk.*
Winston-Derek Publishers, 1990
ISBN: 978-1-55523-296-2
Country/Culture: African American

Motifs: Gardening
Monsters, beasts, or magical creatures

This version stays close to the original, with the addition of African American characters in the illustrations. This time the Jack character, named Jamako, steals only a magic harp and golden goose, which provide Jamako and his mother the means to buy food so they won't be hungry. Along with the text, each illustration is accompanied by a banner describing the scene depicted.

140   DESPAIN, PLEASANT.   *Strongheart Jack and the Beanstalk.*
Ill. by Joe Shlichta. August House Little Folk, 1995
ISBN: 978-0-87483-414-7
Motifs: Gardening
Monsters, beasts, or magical creatures

An extended version of the original story collected by Jacobs. It features the history of the giant's cruelty towards Jack's family (the giant killed and ate Jack's father); a talking cat who follows and protects Jack; altercations with a cactus plant army and a tortoise; and a young girl held captive by the giant. Includes an author's note on the origin of the story.

141   GRANOWSKY, ALVIN.   *Giants Have Feelings, Too.*
Ill. by Henry Buerchkholtz. Steck-Vaughn, 1996
ISBN: 978-0-8114-7129-9
Motifs: Gardening
Monsters, beasts, or magical creatures

Part of the publisher's Point of View series. This edition has the original tale told in the first part, and then the book is turned over to read the other side of the story, narrated by the giant's wife. In her version, Jack is nothing but a common thief who took advantage of the giants when they offered him kindness.

142   HALEY, GAIL E.   *Jack and the Bean Tree.*
Crown, 1986
ISBN: 978-0-517-55717-4
Country/Culture: Appalachia
Motifs: Gardening
Monsters, beasts, or magical creatures

An Appalachian version of the story told in mountain dialect. When Jack comes home with the beans he traded for the cow, his mother throws the beans out Jack's bedroom window and locks him in. He cries out the window, and it is his tears that make the beanstalk grow overnight.

143   HARRIS, JIM.   *Jack and the Giant: A Story Full of Beans.*
Rising Moon, 1997
ISBN: 978-0-87358-680-1
Country/Culture: Western
Motifs: Gardening
      Monsters, beasts, or magical creatures
A cowboy version that has Jack meeting the giant, Wild Bill Hiccup, at his adobe castle in the sky. The giant owns a lasso that turns French fries into gold, a magic singing banjo, and a buffalo that puts out golden buffalo chips. When Wild Bill falls off the beanstalk his impression creates the Grand Canyon.

144   HÉBERT-COLLINS, SHEILA.   *Jacques et la Canne a Sucre: A Cajun Jack and the Beanstalk.*
Ill. by Alison Davis Lyne. Pelican, 2004
ISBN: 978-1-58980-191-2
Country/Culture: Cajun
Motifs: Gardening
Jacques lives in the bayou where he and his mother catch crawfish for a living. On his way to market with the crawfish, Jacques meets an old Cajun who buys the crawfish from him for five dollars and magic sugar cane cuttings. The cuttings turn into a giant stalk of sugar cane when Jacques's mother throws them out the window. Includes definitions and pronunciation guide for French Cajun words on each page, and a recipe for shrimp or crawfish etouffee.

145   HOLUB, JOAN.   *Jack and the Jellybeanstalk.*
Ill. by Benton Mahan. Grosset & Dunlap, 2002
ISBN: 978-0-448-42657-0
Motifs: Gardening
      Animals (rabbits or hares)
      Seasons (spring)
Jack is a bunny who loves jelly beans. He happens upon some magic jelly beans that grow a stalk outside his window. The giant weasel who lives at the top of the jelly bean stalk tries to make Jack into a stew. Jack blows pepper into the giant weasel's face making the weasel sneeze so hard that he blows Jack out of the pot and back home.

146   KETTEMAN, HELEN.   *Waynetta and the Cornstalk: A Texas Fairy Tale.*
Ill. by Diane Greenseid. Albert Whitman, 2007
ISBN: 978-0-8075-8687-7
Country/Culture: Western
Motifs: Farms
      Monsters, beasts, or magical creatures
      Gender role reversal

Waynetta trades their last cow for a handful of magic corn. She climbs the giant cornstalk that grows, and finds a giant ranch that is home to a giant cowboy and his wife. Waynetta manages to steal back the longhorn that lays gold cow patties, a magic lasso that never misses, and a tiny bucket that never empties, which the giant stole from her mother years ago.

147   KURTZ, JOHN.   *Jack and the Beanstalk.*
Jump at the Sun/Hyperion Books for Children, 2004
ISBN: 978-0-7868-0954-7
Country/Culture: African American
Motifs: Gardening
      Monsters, beasts, or magical creatures

In this standard retelling of the original story, the characters have been changed in the illustrations to be African American. Jack sells the cow for beans because he is too lazy to walk to town. When Jack climbs the beanstalk he encounters a fairy who challenges him to prove that he is brave and selfless by returning the giant's treasures to their rightful owner. Part of the Jump at the Sun Fairy-tale Classics series.

148   LAIRD, DONIVEE MARTIN.   *Keaka and the Liliko'i Vine.*
Ill. by Carol Jossem. Barnaby Books, 1982
ISBN: 978-0-940350-06-9
Country/Culture: Hawaii
Motifs: Gardening
      Monsters, beasts, or magical creatures

An account of the original story, set on the island of Hawaii. When Keaka and his mother cannot find enough bananas or fish to eat, they must sell their goat. The beans Keaka trades for it grow a huge vine up to the clouds. At the top, Keaka finds a giant who is hiding a golden-egg-laying nene goose and a magic ukulele that plays by itself, treasures that he stole from Keaka's village. Other changes include the addition of Hawaiian dialect. Includes a glossary of Hawaiian and pidgin words used and a pronunciation guide.

149   OSBORNE, MARY POPE.   *Kate and the Beanstalk.*

Ill. by Giselle Potter. Atheneum, 2000

ISBN: 978-0-689-82550-7

Motifs: Gardening

Monsters, beasts, or magical creatures

Gender role reversal

This version stays close to the original but the protagonist is a girl. Kate does not realize the giant's treasures were stolen from her family, which is why they are poverty stricken now. Kate's mother is the rightful owner of the castle in the sky.

150   PAULSON, TIM.   *The Beanstalk Incident.*

Ill. by Mark Corcoran. Carol Pub. Group, 1990

ISBN: 978-1-55972-048-9

Motifs: Gardening

Monsters, beasts, or magical creatures

This edition has the original story printed on one side and an opposing version narrated by Lucille, the golden-egg-laying goose, on the other. According to Lucille, Jack is nothing but a common thief with poor manners who takes advantage of the giant's kindness. When Alvin, the giant, chases Jack, he is only trying to retrieve his own property.

151   STANLEY, DIANE.   *The Giant and the Beanstalk.*

HarperCollins, 2004

ISBN: 978-0-06-000010-3

Motifs: Monsters, beasts, or magical creatures

Gardening

Animals (cows)

Birds (chickens or roosters)

Told from the giant's viewpoint. The giant is a friendly boy who just wants his favorite pet hen back from Jack. He goes down the beanstalk and finds several Jacks—Jack Spratt, Little Jack Horner, Jack Be Nimble, and so forth. He finally finds the right Jack and they trade Jack's cow for the giant's hen.

152   WILDSMITH, BRIAN, AND REBECCA WILDSMITH.   *Jack and the Meanstalk.*

Knopf, 1994

ISBN: 978-0-679-85810-2

Motifs: Gardening

Ecology

Professor Jack is a scientist who is impatient waiting for his bean plants to grow. He invents a new type of bean that will grow very quickly. Unfortunately, it won't stop growing and grows so tall that it puts a hole in the ozone layer and creates environmental problems on Earth. The animals take it upon themselves to kill the plant and save the planet.

THE LITTLE RED HEN

As published in *Stories to Tell Children: Fifty-Four Stories with Some Suggestions for Telling* by Sara Cone Bryant (George G. Harrap & Co. Ltd., 1918)

THE LITTLE RED HEN WAS IN THE FARMYARD with her chickens, when she found a grain of wheat.

"Who will plant this wheat?" she said.

"Not I," said the Goose.

"Not I," said the Duck.

"I will, then," said the little Red Hen, and she planted the grain of wheat.

When the wheat was ripe she said, "Who will take this wheat to the mill?"

"Not I," said the Goose.

"Not I," said the Duck.

"I will, then," said the little Red Hen, and she took the wheat to the mill.

When she brought the flour home she said, "Who will make some bread with this flour?"

"Not I," said the Goose.

"Not I," said the Duck.

"I will, then," said the little Red Hen.

When the bread was baked, she said, "Who will eat this bread?"

"I will," said the Goose.

"I will," said the Duck.

"No, you won't," said the little Red Hen. "I shall eat it myself. Cluck! cluck!" And she called her chickens to help her.

153 FEARNLEY, JAN. *Mr. Wolf's Pancakes.*
Little Tiger Press, 1999
ISBN: 978-1-888444-76-6
Motifs: Animals (wolves or coyotes)
Food (breads or grains)
Farms

Mr. Wolf asks each of the farm animals to help him make pancakes, but each in turn is unwilling to help and slams the door on him. When the pancakes are done, the animals come to eat them, but the wolf decides that the animals will make a tasty appetizer instead.

154 FLEMING, CANDACE. *Gator Gumbo: A Spicy-Hot Tale.*
Ill. by Sally Anne Lambert. Farrar, Straus and Giroux, 2004
ISBN: 978-0-374-38050-2
Country/Culture: Cajun
Motifs: Animals (alligators or crocodiles)
Food (soup or stew)

Monsieur Gator is getting old and can't catch the swamp varmints like he used to, so they make good fun out of taunting him. One day Gator decides to make gumbo just like his maman used to make. Possum, Otter, and Skunk refuse to help but can't resist getting closer and closer to smell it cook. When they get close enough to taste the gumbo, Monsieur Gator makes *them* the main ingredients.

155 GRANOWSKY, ALVIN. *Help Yourself, Little Red Hen!*
Ill. by Jane K. Manning. Steck-Vaughn, 1996
ISBN: 978-0-8114-7126-8
Motifs: Animals
Food (soup or stew)
Birds (chickens or roosters)

Part of the publisher's Point of View series. This edition has the original tale in the first part, and then the book is turned over to read the other side of the story. In the version narrated by the other farm animals, Little Red Hen is always trying to get others to do her work for her. They are teaching her a lesson by making her do all her own work, and don't mind that she reaps the rewards herself.

156 KANTOR, SUSAN. *Tiny Tilda's Pumpkin Pie.*
Ill. by Rick Brown. Grosset & Dunlap, 2002
ISBN: 978-0-448-42681-5

Tiny Tilda is a large hippopotamus with three lazy sisters, Hilda, Gilda, and Wilda. Tilda usually does all the housework while the others lie about the house. When Tilda finds a pumpkin seed, none of her sisters will help with the planting and harvesting, so Tilda shares the pie with her neighbors, one of whom finances a bake shop for Tilda so she doesn't have to do her sisters' housework any more.

157   KETTEMAN, HELEN. *Armadilly Chili.*

Ill. by Will Terry. Albert Whitman, 2004
ISBN: 978-0-8075-0457-4
Country/Culture: Western
Motifs: Food (soup or stew)
            Animals

Miss Billie Armadilly asks her friends to help her make chili, but each in turn says no. When the chili is finished, Miss Billie can't figure out what is the last ingredient she needs. Then her friends come to the house with apologies and more food, and she realizes it was companionship.

158   MCGRATH, BARBARA BARBIERI. *The Little Green Witch.*

Ill. by Martha G. Alexander. Charlesbridge, 2005
ISBN: 978-1-58089-042-7
Motifs: Holidays (Halloween)
            Food (soup or stew)
            Monsters, beasts, or magical creatures

Little Green Witch asks Bat, Ghost, and Gremlin for help making pumpkin pie but they refuse her requests. When the pie is properly burned the witch sits down to eat. Ghost, Bat, and Gremlin come and ask for something to eat, and she turns them into little red hens for not helping.

159   PAUL, ANN WHITFORD. *Mañana Iguana.*

Ill. by Ethan Long. Holiday House, 2004
ISBN: 978-0-8234-1808-4
Country/Culture: Hispanic
Motifs: Animals (lizards)
            Animals (tortoises or turtles)

Iguana wants to have a party to celebrate spring, but Conejo, Tortuga, and Culebra don't want to help prepare. So Iguana does all the work herself and doesn't let those friends attend. Conejo, Tortuga, and Culebra watch the fiesta from afar, and realize how much work Iguana put into it without their help. To make amends, while Iguana sleeps, they clean up the whole mess. Includes a glossary and pronunciation guide for Spanish words.

160   STEVENS, JANET, AND SUSAN STEVENS CRUMMEL.   *Cook-a-Doodle-Doo!*
Ill. by Janet Stevens. Harcourt Brace, 1999
ISBN: 978-0-15-201924-2
Motifs: Animals
　　　　Food (desserts)
　　　　Birds (chickens or roosters)
　　　　Cooking

When Big Brown Rooster gets tired of chicken feed, he decides to cook strawberry shortcake just like his granny, Little Red Hen. He first asks Cat, Dog, and Goose to help but they refuse. Instead, Turtle, Pig, and Iguana help, learning about cooking and teamwork as they proceed. Includes sidebars that describe the cooking process.

161   STURGES, PHILEMON.   *The Little Red Hen Makes a Pizza.*
Ill. by Amy Walrod. Dutton Children's Books, 1999
ISBN: 978-0-525-45953-8
Motifs: Birds (chickens or roosters)
　　　　Food (pizza)

Little Red Hen repeatedly asks Duck, Cat, and Dog to go to the store and get ingredients to help her make her pizza, but they all refuse. But they are happy to help eat it (and then clean up) when the pizza is too large for Hen to eat herself.

The Pancake

Versions of this story are common in folklore. "The Runaway Pancake" (A-T type 2025) has variants in Russia (Afanas'ev's "The Bun"), England (Jacobs's "Johnny-Cake"), and Germany (Colshorn's "The Thick, Fat Pancake"). It appeared in the American publication *St. Nicholas Magazine* in 1875 as "The Gingerbread Boy." Regardless of its incarnation, the premise remains the same in each. A bread object acquires human attributes when it is baked. Fully cooked, it runs from the baker and various pursuers who wish to eat it. Each time a pursuer is met, the bread-man recites an antagonist rhyme, teasing them to continue the chase. At last he is convinced by one to step closer and closer, and he is devoured. The version presented here is abridged from *English Fairy Tales Collected by Joseph Jacobs* (Third edition, revised. G.P. Putnam's Sons, 1902).

JOHNNY-CAKE

ONCE UPON A TIME THERE WAS AN OLD MAN, and an old woman, and a little boy. One morning the old woman made a Johnny-cake, and put it in the oven to bake. The old man and the old woman went out and left the boy to tend the oven. The boy heard a noise, and out of the oven jumped the Johnny-cake, rolling along end over end, out the open door. The little boy ran after him as fast as he could, crying out to his father and mother, and they gave chase. But the Johnny-cake outran all three, and was soon out of sight.

On went Johnny-cake, until he came to two well-diggers who called out: "Where are you going, Johnny-cake?"

He said:

"I've outrun an old man,
and an old woman, and a little boy,
and I can outrun you too-o-o!"

"You can, can you? We'll see about that!" they said and threw down their picks and ran after him, but couldn't catch up.

On ran Johnny-cake, and by-and-by he came to two ditch-diggers. "Where are you going, Johnny-cake?" said they.

He said:

"I've outrun an old man,

and an old woman, and a little boy,

and two well-diggers,

and I can outrun you too-o-o!"

"You can, can you? We'll see about that!" they said and threw down their spades, and ran after him too. But Johnny-cake soon outstripped them also.

On went Johnny-cake, and by-and-by he came to a bear. The bear said: "Where are you going, Johnny-cake?"

He said:

"I've outrun an old man,

and an old woman, and a little boy,

and two well-diggers, and two ditch-diggers,

and I can outrun you too-o-o!"

"You can, can you?" growled the bear, "we'll see about that!" and trotted as fast as his legs could carry him after Johnny-cake. But before long the bear too was left far behind.

By-and-by Johnny-cake came to a wolf. The wolf said, "Where are you going, Johnny-cake?"

And Johnny-cake replied,

"I've outrun an old man,

and an old woman, and a little boy,

and two well-diggers, and two ditch-diggers

and a bear, and I can outrun you too-o-o!"

"You can, can you?" snarled the wolf, "we'll see about that!" And he set into a gallop, but soon saw there was no hope of overtaking him.

On went Johnny-cake, and by-and-by he came to a fox. The fox called out in a sharp voice, "Where are you going, Johnny-cake?"

"I've outrun an old man,

and an old woman, and a little boy,

and two well-diggers, and two ditch-diggers,

a bear and a wolf,

and I can outrun you too-o-o!" Johnny-cake sang.

The fox turned his head a little to one side and said, "I can't quite hear you, boy, come a little closer."

Johnny-cake stopped his running and went a little closer. He called out in a very loud voice,

"I've outrun an old man,

and an old woman, and a little boy,

and two well-diggers, and two ditch-diggers,

a bear and a wolf,

and I can outrun you too-o-o!"

"I still can't hear you; won't you come a *little* closer?" said the fox in a feeble voice. He put one paw behind his ear.

Johnny-cake crept up close to the fox and screamed:
"I'VE OUTRUN AN OLD MAN,
AND AN OLD WOMAN, AND A LITTLE BOY,
AND TWO WELL-DIGGERS, AND TWO DITCH-DIGGERS,
AND A BEAR, AND A WOLF,
AND I CAN OUTRUN YOU TOO-O-O!"
"You can, can you?" yelped the fox, and he snapped him up in his sharp teeth in the twinkling of an eye. And that was the end of the Johnny-cake.

---

162   AMOSS, BERTHE. *The Cajun Gingerbread Boy.*

Hyperion, 1994
ISBN: 978-1-78680-114-2
Country/Culture: Cajun
Motifs: Food (desserts)
       Animals (alligators or crocodiles)
       Music (zydeco)
       Cooking

A Cajun grandma bakes a gingerbread boy to keep her company. When she opens the oven he runs out of the house and into the swamp. He runs away from a shrimp fisherman, a zydeco fiddler, and a sugarcane farmer before asking an alligator for help crossing the bayou. Includes a cutout gingerbread boy with slots to fit in each of the pages.

163   ARMOUR, PETER. *Stop That Pickle!*

Ill. by Andrew Shachat. Houghton Mifflin, 1993
ISBN: 978-0-395-66375-2
Motifs: Food

A pickle jumps out of his jar and runs away from the woman who wants to eat him. As he runs he is chased by an apple, a pretzel, almonds, raisins, a doughnut, and grape juice. The pickle runs right into a hungry little boy who decides all the food will make a tasty meal.

164   AYLESWORTH, JIM. *The Gingerbread Man.*

Ill. by Barbara McClintock. Scholastic, 1998
ISBN: 978-0-590-97219-2
Motifs: Food (desserts)
       Animals (foxes)

A little old man and woman bake a gingerbread boy to keep them company. When they open the oven he jumps out and escapes into the forest. He outruns a butcher, a cow, and a pig before he reaches the river and the fox. Rather than helping the cookie to cross the river, the fox pretends he can't hear, and lures him closer and closer until the fox can snap him up.

165   BRETT, JAN.   *Gingerbread Baby.*

Putnam, 1999
ISBN: 978-0-399-23444-6
Motifs: Food (desserts)
Cooking

The pancake is a gingerbread cookie baked by a boy. Mattie opens the door to the oven too soon releasing the gingerbread baby, who goes on a run. While he is out running, Mattie builds a gingerbread house for him to return to.

166   BROWN, MARCIA.   *The Bun: A Tale from Russia.*

Harcourt Brace Jovanovich, 1972
ISBN: 978-0-15-213450-1
Country/Culture: Russia
Motifs: Food (breads or grains)
Animals (foxes)

This account is set in Russia. When the little old woman opens the stove, the bun jumps out and heads into the forest. He outruns several animals before the fox convinces him that he is too deaf to hear what the bun is saying and lures him close enough to be eaten.

167   COMPESTINE, YING CHANG.   *The Runaway Rice Cake.*

Ill. by Tungwai Chau. Simon & Schuster, 2001
ISBN: 978-0-689-82972-7
Country/Culture: China
Motifs: Food (breads or grains)
Holidays (Chinese New Year)
Cooking

When the Chinese New Year comes, the hungry Chang family has only enough rice flour for one rice cake. But when they open the pan, the cake jumps out and runs away, shouting "Ai yo! I don't think so!" They chase it all over town until it knocks over an old lady. The family decides to share the cake with the old woman, and when they return to their home, the Kitchen God rewards them for their generosity.

168   ERNST, LISA CAMPBELL.   *The Gingerbread Girl.*
Dutton Children's Books, 2006
ISBN: 978-0-525-47667-2
Motifs: Gender role reversal
Food (desserts)
Cooking

The Gingerbread Girl is the younger sibling of the Gingerbread Boy. She is determined to prove she is smarter and more clever than her brother. She leads all her chasers, including the fox, back to the old man and woman's house and cooks dinner for everyone.

169   HASSETT, JOHN, AND ANN HASSETT.   *Can't Catch Me.*
Houghton Mifflin, 2006
ISBN: 978-0-618-70490-3
Motifs: Oceans or sealife

An ice cube escapes from the freezer and runs past a little boy, an ant, a dog, and others on his way to the sea to become an iceberg. When he gets to the sea, a whale convinces him that there are boats that the ice cube can bump into in the whale's belly. The ice cube goes into the whale and is never heard from again.

170   HOWLAND, NAOMI.   *The Matzah Man: A Passover Story.*
Clarion Books, 2002
ISBN: 978-0-618-11750-5
Country/Culture: Jewish
Motifs: Holidays (Passover)
Food (breads or grains)
Cooking

The matzah man jumps out of Mr. Cohen's oven and runs away from people who want him to be part of their seder. Finally, he runs into Mendel Fox's house, and Mendel convinces him to hide under the matzah cover until the meal is ready. When Seder begins, the matzah man is eaten as part of the supper. Includes a glossary of Passover terms.

171   JONES, CAROL.   *The Gingerbread Man.*
Houghton Mifflin, 2002
ISBN: 978-0-618-18822-2
Motifs: Food (desserts)
Cooking

This cookie boy runs through the woods and past other storybook characters. Humpty Dumpty, Little Boy Blue, the Little Old Woman Who

Lived in a Shoe, the Grand Duke of York, and Little Miss Muffet all chase him until he gets to the river and meets Sly Fox.

172   KIMMEL, ERIC A.   *The Runaway Tortilla.*

Ill. by Randy Cecil. Winslow Press, 2000
ISBN: 978-1-890817-18-3
Country/Culture: Hispanic
Motifs: Cowboys
         Cooking
         Food (breads or grains)
         Animals (wolves or coyotes)

On a southwestern ranch, Tia Lupé and Tio José bake a tortilla that is lighter and fluffier than any they have made before. When they open the oven, it jumps out and runs away. The tortilla rolls through the desert, eluding horned toads, donkeys, jackrabbits, rattlesnakes, and buckaroos, but is finally outsmarted by Señor Coyote.

173   KIMMELMAN, LESLIE.   *The Runaway Latkes.*

Ill. by Paul Yalowitz. Albert Whitman, 2000
ISBN: 978-0-8075-7176-7
Country/Culture: Jewish
Motifs: Cooking
         Food (breads or grains)
         Holidays (Hanukkah)

On the first night of Hanukkah Rebecca fries latkes. When the latkes are cooked, they jump out of the pan. After an extended chase that involves everyone from the synagogue, the latkes end up in the town river, which turns to applesauce. Finally caught, and perfectly covered with applesauce, they are eaten by their pursuers.

174   KIRK, DANIEL.   *Snow Dude.*

Hyperion Books for Children, 2004
ISBN: 978-0-7868-1942-3
Motifs: Sports (snowboarding)
         Seasons (winter)

Two children build a cool snowboarding snowman who comes to life and runs away. He is chased by a variety of people and animals who want to catch him for the snowman competition. When he reaches a frozen river bank and can go no further, the children show them all how to make snow dudes of their own.

175 LITHGOW, JOHN. *Marsupial Sue Presents the Runaway Pancake.*
Ill. by Jack E. Davis. Simon & Schuster, 2005
ISBN: 978-0-689-87847-3
Motifs: Food (breads or grains)
Animals (foxes)

This adaptation is presented as a play put on by the characters of "Marsupial Sue." Their version does not end with the pancake being eaten. Instead, the animals who pursued the pancake get angry at the fox for eating their lunch and chase him out of the forest.

176 OPPENHEIM, JOANNE. *You Can't Catch Me!*
Ill. by Andrew Shachat. Houghton Mifflin, 1986
ISBN: 978-0-395-41452-1
Motifs: Animals

A pesky black fly spends all day annoying the animals in and around the farm. He slaps the cow, bothers the goat, pesters the horse, and buzzes the bear, teasing each one because they can't catch him. In the evening he settles down to sleep on what he thinks is a rock, but it is actually a hungry turtle who can catch him.

177 PALATINI, MARGIE. *Bad Boys Get Cookie!*
Ill. by Henry Cole. Katherine Tegen Books, 2006
ISBN: 978-0-06-074436-6
Motifs: Food (desserts)
Animals (wolves or coyotes)

Willis and Wallace Wolf are really, really bad boys who are pretending to be detectives to help the baker find his runaway cookie. They dress up as Hansel and Gretel and the Gingerbread Boy leads them on a chase, finally ending up at the old witch's cottage made of sweets. The ending is unclear as to who gets who; the wolves eat the witch or the witch cooks the wolves.

178 POMERANTZ, CHARLOTTE. *Whiff, Sniff, Nibble, and Chew: The Gingerbread Boy Retold.*
Ill. by Monica Incisa. Greenwillow Books, 1984
ISBN: 978-0-688-02551-9
Motifs: Food (desserts)
Animals

After being chased around the woods by the animals, the cookie boy returns home only to be eaten by the old man. That night he escapes from the old man's stomach, and he and the old woman run away together. Later they meet a kind man who has a gingerbread daughter. They get married and live happily ever after as a family.

179 SHULMAN, LISA. *The Matzo Ball Boy.*
Ill. by Rosanne Litzinger. Dutton Children's Books, 2005
ISBN: 978-0-525-47169-1
Country/Culture: Jewish
Motifs: Cooking
      Food (breads or grains)
      Holidays (Passover)
      Food (soup or stew)

The matzo ball boy runs away from the old woman who made him, the rabbi, the yenti, and others preparing for the holiday. He even gets away from the fox at the river by swimming it himself. Toward evening he meets a poor man in the woods who invites him to his cottage, and the poor man and his wife have matzo ball soup for Passover. Includes author's note on Passover and a glossary of Yiddish and Hebrew terms.

180 SQUIRES, JANET. *The Gingerbread Cowboy.*
Ill. by Holly Berry. Laura Geringer Books, 2006
ISBN: 978-0-06-077863-7
Country/Culture: Western
Motifs: Cowboys
      Animals (wolves or coyotes)
      Food (desserts)
      Cooking

The rancher's wife is tired of making biscuits every day, so one day she makes something different, a gingerbread cowboy. When she tries to take him out of the oven, he runs away from the ranchers, a roadrunner, a band of javelinas, long-horned cattle, and some hungry cowboys, but he can't escape the coyote who volunteers to help him across the river.

181 TAKAYAMA, SANDI. *The Musubi Man: Hawai'i's Gingerbread Man.*
Ill. by Pat Hall. Bess Press, 1996
ISBN: 978-1-57306-053-0
Country/Culture: Hawaii
Motifs: Food (breads or grains)
      Sports (surfing)

Musubi Man is made of sushi ingredients. He runs across the island chased by the old woman and old man, a dog, a mynah bird and a mongoose until he catches a ride with a surfer. The surfer decides Musubi Man is good luck, so he turns pro and wins international competitions. Includes a glossary of Hawai'ian food.

182   TAKAYAMA, SANDI. *The Musubi Man's New Friend.*
Ill. by Pat Hall. Bess Press, 2002
ISBN: 978-1-57306-144-5
Country/Culture: Hawaii
Motifs: Food (desserts)
　　　　　Sports (surfing)

This is a sequel to *The Musubi Man* (see above). Surfer teaches Musubi Man to surf and makes him his own surfboard. Each time Musubi Man goes surfing, a hungry creature tries to capture him for a meal, but he runs away laughing. When Musubi Man gets tired of being chased and wants to quit surfing, Surfer decides to make him a special friend and creates Musubi Girl with a heart made of SPAM.

THE PRINCESS AND THE PEA

Published as "The Real Princess" in *Stories from Hans Andersen* (Hodder & Stoughton, 1911).

THE REAL PRINCESS

THERE WAS ONCE A PRINCE, AND HE WANTED A PRINCESS, but she must be a *real* Princess. He traveled right round the world to find one, but there was always something wrong. There were plenty of princesses, but whether they were real princesses he had great difficulty in discovering; there was always something which was not quite right about them. So at last he had to come home again, and he was very sad because he wanted a real princess so badly.

One evening there was a terrible storm; it thundered and lightened and the rain poured down in torrents; indeed it was a fearful night.

In the middle of the storm somebody knocked at the town gate, and the old King himself went to open it.

It was a princess who stood outside, but she was in a terrible state from the rain and the storm. The water streamed out of her hair and her clothes; it ran in at the top of her shoes and out at the heel, but she said that she was a real princess.

"Well we shall soon see if that is true," thought the old Queen, but she said nothing. She went into the bedroom, took all the bedclothes off and laid a pea on the bedstead: then she took twenty mattresses and piled them on the top of the pea, and then twenty feather beds on the top of the mattresses. This was where the princess was to sleep that night. In the morning they asked her how she had slept.

"Oh terribly badly!" said the princess. "I have hardly closed my eyes the whole night! Heaven knows what was in the bed. I seemed to be lying upon some hard thing, and my whole body is black and blue this morning. It is terrible!"

They saw at once that she must be a real princess when she had felt the pea through twenty mattresses and twenty feather beds. Nobody but a real princess could have such a delicate skin.

So the prince took her to be his wife, for now he was sure that he had found a real princess, and the pea was put into the Museum, where it may still be seen if no one has stolen it.

Now this is a true story.

183   AUCH, MARY JANE.   *The Princess and the Pizza.*

Ill. by Herm Auch. Holiday House, 2002
ISBN: 978-0-8234-1683-7
Motifs: Food (pizza)
Fruits and vegetables (peas)

The king gives up his throne to become a woodcarver, but his daughter, Princess Paulina, thinks she misses the royal life. She signs up for a cooking contest to marry a prince, but is sabotaged by the other contestants. The only food she can make with the ingredients that she has is pizza. Prince Drupert loves it and she wins the contest. Ultimately, she realizes that she would rather cook pizzas than marry Drupert, and opens her own pizza parlor.

184   CAMPBELL, ANN.   *Once Upon a Princess and a Pea.*

Ill. by Kathy Osborn Young. Stewart, Tabori & Chang, 1993
ISBN: 978-1-55670-289-1
Motifs: Fruits and vegetables (peas)

Princess Esmerelda runs away from home when she learns that her parents want her to marry the old King Frobius. One rainy night she meets Prince Hector, who is out trying to find a suitable princess to marry. He brings Esmerelda home, but she is so bedraggled that she has to prove to his mother that she is a real princess.

185   GREY, MINI.   *The Very Smart Pea and the Princess-to-Be.*

Knopf, 2003
ISBN: 978-0-375-82626-9

Motifs: Fruits and vegetables (peas)
Gardening

This version is told from the pea's point of view. The pea tells how one night her gardener took refuge from a storm in the prince's home. She slept on a pile of mattresses under which the pea was hidden. The pea wiggled to the top of the mattress pile while the gardener slept and whispered that there was something "Large Round and Uncomfortable" under the mattress. When the gardener complained of this the next morning, the prince's mother is convinced that she is a real princess and insists that the gardener marry her son.

186   JOHNSTON, TONY.   *The Cowboy and the Black-Eyed Pea.*
Ill. by Warren Ludwig. Putnam, 1992
ISBN: 978-0-399-22330-3
Country/Culture: Western
Motifs: Cowboys
Fruits and vegetables (peas)
Gender role reversal

Farethee Well, the daughter of a rich rancher, wants to find a real cowboy to marry. To test each suitor she puts a black-eyed pea under his saddle and sends him out to gather the herd. When twenty saddle blankets cannot hide the pea from one of the suitors, she knows she has found her true love.

187   NIKLY, MICHELLE.   *The Princess on the Nut: Or, the Curious Courtship of the Son of the Princess on the Pea.*
Ill. by Jean Claverie. Faber and Faber, 1981
ISBN: 978-0-571-11846-5
Motifs: Fruits and vegetables (peas)
Gender role reversal
Food (nuts)

In this adaptation the prince is the son of the princess from the "Princess and the Pea." When he goes looking for a bride, all the prince finds are perfect princesses. He decides he is bored with perfect people and looks for someone who will do the unexpected.

188   PERLMAN, JANET.   *The Penguin and the Pea.*
Kids Can Press, 2004
ISBN: 978-1-55074-832-1
Motifs: Birds (penguins)
Fruits and vegetables (cabbage or lettuce)
Fruits and vegetables (peas)

The penguin princess must pass two tests. First, the queen puts a cabbage under her mattress, but the princess is too polite to mention it. When the prince insists that he is going to marry her, the queen puts the pea under twenty mattresses. When the princess admits at breakfast that she is sore all over, the prince knows that they will live "flappily" ever after.

189   TAKAYAMA, SANDI.   *The Prince and Li Hing Mui.*
Ill. by Esther Szegedy. Bess Press, 1998
ISBN: 978-1-57306-077-6
Country/Culture: Hawaii
Motifs: Fruits and vegetables (plums)
       Gender role reversal

In this version of the pea story, the princess is looking for a mate. Instead of a pea, the princess and her mother put a li hing mui, a preserved plum, under the guest mattress. The hapless boy who visits while trying to get out of a storm is so polite that he refuses to complain about the lump under the bed. When the princess finds out that he has instead been sleeping on the floor, she decides to marry him.

190   THALER, MIKE.   *The Princess and the Pea-ano.*
Ill. by Jared D. Lee. Scholastic, 1997
ISBN: 978-0-590-89825-6
Motifs: Fruits and vegetables (peas)

The king and queen run a bed and breakfast where many princesses stay the night. None can feel the pea that the queen puts under her mattress, no matter what the prince does to try to disturb their sleep. Finally, the prince puts a piano under one princess's mattress, but even that doesn't wake her because she is Sleeping Beauty. Part of the Happily Ever Laughter series.

191   VAES, ALAIN.   *The Princess and the Pea.*
Little, Brown, 2001
ISBN: 978-0-316-89633-7
Motifs: Transportation (trucks)
       Jewelry

Princess Opal is driving a tow truck and picks up the distraught prince after his vehicle breaks down. The queen's plan to show that Opal isn't really a princess fails when Opal's necklace gets caught in her hair before bedtime. Opal sleeps on the necklace all night, which gives her bruises, and demonstrates that she really is royalty.

192 WILSDORF, ANNE. *Princess.*
Greenwillow Books, 1993
ISBN: 978-0-688-11541-8
Motifs: Fruits and vegetables (peas)

The princesses that the prince finds are either too busy watching television, too neat, or too bloodthirsty for his taste. On the way back to the castle he meets a shepherd girl named Princess and immediately falls in love with her. When the queen puts her to the pea test, Princess falls out of bed during the night and gets all bruised, thereby demonstrating that she is worthy of marrying the prince.

RAPUNZEL

Abridged from *Household Stories by the Brothers Grimm* (Macmillan and Company, 1886).

HERE ONCE LIVED A MAN AND HIS WIFE who were waiting the birth of their first child. Their house had a window that overlooked a beautiful garden. No one ventured there, for it belonged to a great witch. One day the wife looked out the window and saw the garden filled with rampion and she wished for some. She pined away for days, and grew weak. This made her husband uneasy, and he asked, "What is the matter, wife?"

"I will die unless I get some of that rampion from the witch's garden," she replied.

Her husband thought to himself, "Rather than lose my wife I will get some rampion, whatever the cost."

That night he went into the garden, and brought rampion to his wife. She ate it at once, and liked it so much that she longed for more. So her husband went again, but as he was climbing back, the witch stood before him.

"How dare you steal my rampion!" she screamed.

"Be merciful!" replied the man. "My wife saw your rampion, and longed for it so that she would die if she could not have some." Then the witch said, "Then you may have it, but when the child is born, it will be mine."

Fearful, the man agreed. And so when the child was born the witch took her, naming her Rapunzel, which means rampion.

When she was twelve years old the witch shut Rapunzel up in a tower with no door or steps, only a small window. When the witch wanted in, she would stand below and cry, "Rapunzel, Rapunzel! Let down your hair!"

Rapunzel had beautiful long golden hair. When the witch called, Rapunzel would open the window, unbind her braids, and let it down, and the witch would climb up by it.

It happened one day that the King's son was riding through the wood. When he came to the tower he heard Rapunzel singing sweetly, trying to pass away the time with songs. The Prince wished to find her, but could not find a door in the tower. So he returned every day to listen to the singing. One day he saw the witch call out,

"Rapunzel, Rapunzel! Let down your hair."

The prince saw how the witch entered the tower, and he said to himself,

"I must climb that ladder." And the next evening he went to the tower and cried,

"Rapunzel, Rapunzel! Let down your hair."

Rapunzel let down her hair, and the King's son climbed up to her.

Rapunzel was frightened by the Prince, but he spoke to her kindly and told her how her singing had touched his heart. So Rapunzel forgot her terror, and when he asked her to marry him, she said,

"I would go with you, but I can't get out. When you visit, bring pieces of rope, and I will make a ladder. When it is ready I will use it to climb down and I will go with you." And they agreed that he would come every evening. So it went and the witch knew nothing of it until once Rapunzel said to her unwittingly,

"Witch, how is it that you climb so slowly, but the King's son is so quick?"

"O wicked child," cried the witch, "what is this I hear! You have betrayed me!"

In her anger she seized Rapunzel by her hair, and grasping a pair of shears—snip, snap—the beautiful locks lay on the ground. Then she took Rapunzel and put her in a deserted place, where she lived in great misery.

That same day the witch went back to the tower and tied the severed locks of hair to the window-sill. That night when the Prince came and cried,

"Rapunzel, Rapunzel! let down your hair."

The witch let the hair down, and the King's son climbed up, but he found the witch staring at him with wicked eyes.

"Aha! You came for your song bird, but she is not here. The cat has gotten her, and she sings no more. Rapunzel is lost to you."

In his grief, the Prince sprang from the tower. He did not die, but fell upon a thorn bush which blinded him. And so he wandered through the wood lamenting the loss of his Rapunzel.

At last he came to the deserted place where the witch left Rapunzel. When he heard the voice he thought he knew, he fell on the ground and wept. Rapunzel found him there, and cried for him too. But when her tears touched his eyes he could see with them as well as ever.

Then he took her to his kingdom, and they lived long and happily.

193 BASILE, GIAMBATTISTA, AND JOHN EDWARD TAYLOR. *Petrosinella: A Neapolitan Rapunzel.*
Ill. by Diane Stanley. F. Warne, 1981
ISBN: 978-0-7232-6196-4
Country/Culture: Italy
Motifs: Hair
　　　　Monsters, beasts, or magical creatures

Petrosinella is imprisoned in a tower by an ogress. When she falls in love with a prince they use three magic acorns to aid in their escape. As the ogress chases the couple, the first acorn turns into a large dog, but the ogress gives it a loaf of bread. The second acorn turns into a lion, but the ogress changes herself into a donkey, and the lion is startled and runs away. The last acorn becomes a wolf, which immediately eats the ogress, still in the form of a donkey. The same illustrations are used in a later version with text by Diane Stanley (entry 196).

194 CRUMP, FRED H. *Rapunzel.*
Winston-Derek Publishers, 1991
ISBN: 978-1-55523-408-9
Country/Culture: Africa
Motifs: Hair
　　　　Monsters, beasts, or magical creatures

Rapunzel is an African girl stolen from her parents and held captive in a tower by a witch. Prince Komandi sees Rapunzel and falls in love. He climbs up to see her and together they plan Rapunzel's escape. The witch finds them, cuts off Rapunzel's hair, blinds Komandi, and throws him to the ground. Looking at the injured prince, the witch falls from the tower and is killed. Rapunzel uses her long braids to make a ladder to climb down to the prince. Her grief heals his injuries.

195 ROBERTS, LYNN. *Rapunzel: A Groovy Fairy Tale.*
Ill. by David Roberts. Harry N. Abrams, 2003
ISBN: 978-0-8109-4242-4
Motifs: Hair
　　　　Music (rock)

Set in a contemporary city. Rapunzel is held captive in an apartment by her Aunt Esme, who is also the local school's lunch lady. Roger is the boy who finds her, but when Esme finds out about him, she throws Rapunzel out of the apartment and pushes Roger out of the window. His fall wipes out his memory of Rapunzel until she shows up at his band concert.

196   STANLEY, DIANE.   *Petrosinella: A Neapolitan Rapunzel.*
Dial Books, 1995
ISBN: 978-0-08-037171-9
Country/Culture: Italy
Motifs: Hair
   Monsters, beasts, or magical creatures

Petrosinella, whose name means parsley, is kept in a tower by an ogress. When the prince starts visiting Petrosinella, a nosy neighbor tells the ogress. The ogress casts a spell on the tower, allowing Petrosinella to leave only if she finds three magic acorns she has hidden. The couple finds the acorns and uses them to aid in their escape from the ogress. The same illustrations are used in an earlier version with text by Giambattista Basile and adapted by John Edward Taylor (entry 193).

197   STORACE, PATRICIA.   *Sugar Cane: A Caribbean Rapunzel.*
Ill. by Raul Colon. Jump at the Sun/Hyperion Books for Children, 2007
ISBN: 978-0-7868-0791-8
Country/Culture: Caribbean
Motifs: Music
   Monsters, beasts, or magical creatures
   Hair

Set in the Caribbean. Sugar Cane is named after the sweet treat her father stole to satisfy his pregnant wife's cravings. On her first birthday, Madame Fate, the sorceress who owns the cane field, takes the child as punishment for the theft. Locked in a tower in the jungle, a man named King finds her. They fall in love, and Sugar Cane escapes the tower to be with him and also finds her parents.

198   VOZAR, DAVID.   *Rapunzel: A Happenin' Rap.*
Ill. by Betsy Lewin. Doubleday Books for Young Readers, 1998
ISBN: 978-0-385-32314-7
Country/Culture: African American
Motifs: Hair
   Music (rap or hip-hop)
   Animals (dogs)

Set in a modern city, this version is written as a rap song and the characters are all dogs. Because her father insulted the neighborhood witch, Rapunzel is locked in an upstairs apartment until she is a teen. When she is at last rescued by Fine Prince, she becomes a cosmetologist.

199   WILCOX, LEAH. *Falling for Rapunzel.*
Ill. by Lydia Monks. Putnam, 2003
ISBN: 978-0-399-23794-2
Motifs: Hair

This version is told in rhyme. The prince repeatedly asks Rapunzel to throw down her hair, but the tower is too high for her to hear him correctly. She tosses out a variety of objects, including underwear, socks, and finally her maid, whom the prince decides is a much better catch after all.

RED RIDING HOOD

A longer version can be found in Grimm, with the title "Little Red-Cap." That story does not end with the wolf eating young Red, but introduces a hunter who discovers the wolf asleep, cuts him open, and rescues both the girl and her grandmother in fine shape. Later, Red-Cap returns to grandmother's house and is again approached by a wolf. Undeterred, she goes straight to the cottage. The wolf waits on the roof for her to leave, but her grandmother fills the outside trough with boiling sausage water. The wolf smells the sausage and falls down into the trough and drowns. The version below is adapted from *The Tales of Mother Goose as First Collected by Charles Perrault in 1696* (D.C. Heath & Co., 1901).

LITTLE RED RIDING HOOD

ONCE UPON A TIME THERE LIVED A LITTLE COUNTRY GIRL, the prettiest creature ever seen. Her mother was very fond of her, and her grandmother loved her more, and made for her a little red riding-hood, which was so becoming that everybody called her Little Red Riding-hood.

One day her mother made some custards and said to her,

"Go and see how your grandmother is, for I hear she is ill. Give her a custard and this pot of butter."

So Little Red Riding-hood set out.

As she walked through the wood she met Gaffer Wolf, who wanted to eat her up. But he didn't dare because woodsmen were nearby. He asked Little Red Riding-hood where she was going. The child said to him, "I am going to see my grandmother, and give her this food from my mamma."

"Does she live far off?" asked the Wolf.

"Oh, yes," answered Little Red Riding-hood, "it is beyond the mill."

"Well," said the Wolf, " I'll go and see her, too. I'll go this way, and you go that, and we shall see who will be there first."

The Wolf ran as fast as he could, taking the shortest route, and the little girl went by the longest way, amusing herself by gathering nuts, running after butterflies, and picking flowers. The Wolf quickly reached the old woman's house. He knocked at the door, tap, tap, tap.

"Who's there?" called the grandmother.

"Your grandchild, Little Red Riding-hood," replied the Wolf, imitating her voice, "I have brought a custard and some butter from my mamma."

The good grandmother, who was in bed because she was ill, cried out, "Pull the bobbin, and the latch will go up."

The Wolf opened the door, fell upon the good woman and ate her up. He then shut the door, got into the grandmother's bed, and waited for Little Red Riding-hood. Sometime afterward she knocked at the door, tap, tap, tap.

"Who's there?" called the Wolf.

Little Red Riding-hood, hearing the big voice of the Wolf, was at first afraid; but thinking her grandmother had a cold, answered:-

"It is me, Little Red Riding-hood. I have brought you food from my mamma."

The Wolf cried out to her, softening his voice a little, "Pull the bobbin, and the latch will go up."

So Little Red Riding-hood opened the door and went in.

Seeing her, the Wolf hid himself under the bedclothes. "Put the food on the table, and come lie down with me."

Little Red Riding-hood got into the bed, where she was much surprised to see how her grandmother looked.

She said to her, "Grandmamma, what long arms you have!"

"The better to hug you with, my dear."

"Grandmamma, what long legs you have!"

"The better to run with, my dear."

"Grandmamma, what large ears you have!"

"The better to hear you with, my dear."

"Grandmamma, what great eyes you have!"

"The better to see you with, my dear."

"Grandmamma, what big teeth you have!"

"The better to *eat* you with, my dear!"

And with that, the Wolf fell upon Little Red Riding-hood, and ate her all up.

200   ARTELL, MIKE.   *Petite Rouge: A Cajun Red Riding Hood.*
Ill. by Jim Harris. Dial Books for Young Readers, 2001
ISBN: 978-0-8037-2514-0
Country/Culture: Cajun
Motifs: Animals (alligators or crocodiles)
          Food

This adaptation is told in Cajun dialect and rhyme. The antagonist is an alligator, and the setting is a swamp. When Petite Rouge meets the gator in granny's house, she fends him off by feeding him a boudin sausage soaked in Tabasco. The meat is so hot the gator flees the house and runs back to the swamp with his mouth open to cool off. Includes a glossary and pronunciation guide of French/Cajun words and a brief history of the Cajuns.

201   DALY, NIKI.   *Pretty Salma: A Little Red Riding Hood Story from Africa.*
Clarion Books, 2007
ISBN: 978-0-618-72345-4
Country/Culture: Africa
Motifs: Animals (dogs)

Granny sends Little Salma to the marketplace to buy food. On her way home, Salma meets Mr. Dog. He talks Salma out of her clothing and packages and heads to Granny's house dressed as Salma. Salma runs away and tells Grandpa, and the two of them dress up as Anansi the Spider and Ka Ka Motobi the Bogeyman to scare Dr. Dog. Includes pronunciation guide and translation of Ghanaian words.

202   EMBERLEY, MICHAEL.   *Ruby.*
Little, Brown, 1990
ISBN: 978-0-316-23643-0
Motifs: Animals (cats)
          Animals (mice)
          Animals (dogs)

Ruby is a mouse whose mother warns her to never talk to cats. On her way to Granny's house, Ruby does talk to a very slick cat, who grabs a taxi to get to Granny's first. The cat doesn't count on Granny Mouse's neighbor, Mrs. Mastiff, who opens the door for him.

203   ERNST, LISA CAMPBELL.   *Little Red Riding Hood: A Newfangled Prairie Tale.*
Simon & Schuster, 1995
ISBN: 978-0-689-80145-7
Country/Culture: Midwest
Motifs: Farms
            Animals (wolves or coyotes)

An updated version set in midwestern corn fields. Red Riding Hood goes on her bicycle to deliver muffins to her Granny, but is stopped on the way by a wolf. Wanting all the muffins and the recipe for himself, the wolf gets to Granny's first. However, he hasn't counted on meeting a Granny with an attitude, and she easily puts him in his place.

204   FORWARD, TOBY.   *The Wolf's Story: What Really Happened to Little Red Riding Hood.*
Ill. by Izhar Cohen. Walker, 2005
ISBN: 978-1-4063-0162-5
Motifs: Animals (wolves or coyotes)

This adaptation is told from the wolf's point of view. He insists that he was a completely innocent and trustworthy handyman for Grandma. He was trying to help Grandma get her robe out of the closet when she knocked herself out, and he panicked and pretended to be her because he knew Red would think the worst of him if she found Grandma like that. It was fate that conspired against him to make him look guilty.

205   HÉBERT-COLLINS, SHEILA.   *Petite Rouge: A Cajun Twist to an Old Tale.*
Ill. by Chris Diket. Pelican, 1997
ISBN: 978-1-56554-310-2
Country/Culture: Cajun
Motifs: Food (soup or stew)
            Animals (alligators or crocodiles)

This account is the traditional tale, but told with Cajun details. The wolf is an alligator, a swamp is the setting, and the girl's gift that she carries to her grandmother is shrimp etouffee. When the gator swallows Petite Rouge, shrimp fishermen hear her scream and catch the alligator. The men slice open the gator and out pop Grandmere and Petite Rouge in fine shape. That night the gator is dinner at a Cajun party. Includes French/Cajun words translated with pronunciations on each page. Includes recipe for alligator sauce piquante.

206   JACKSON, BOBBY.   *Little Red Ronnika.*

Ill. by Rhonda Mitchell. Multicultural Publications, 1998

ISBN: 978-1-884242-80-9

Country/Culture: African American

Motifs: Transportation (cars)

Animals (wolves or coyotes)

Ronnika is an African American girl living in contemporary Ohio. Granny, who drives a red Lamborghini, does not take well to the wolf at her door and whacks him with a frying pan. Although she and Ronnika do get eaten, they are set free by a passing tree trimmer. In the end they eat wolf meat for a week, Granny gets a silver wolf fur coat, and they all go for a spin in the sports car.

207   KURTZ, JOHN.   *Little Red Riding Hood.*

Jump at the Sun/Hyperion Books for Children, 2004

ISBN: 978-0-7868-0953-0

Country/Culture: African American

Motifs: Animals (wolves or coyotes)

In this standard retelling of the original story, the characters are portrayed as African American. The wolf does not eat the grandma because she is smart enough to run away. She escapes out the back door and gets the woodsman, Red's mother, and some townsfolk to chase the wolf out of the house. Part of the Jump at the Sun Fairy-tale Classics series.

208   LAIRD, DONIVEE MARTIN.   *'Ula Li'i and the Magic Shark.*

Ill. by Carol Jossem. Barnaby Books, 1985

ISBN: 978-0-940350-09-0

Country/Culture: Hawaii

Motifs: Fish (sharks)

An account of Red Riding Hood set in Hawaii. A magic shark sent to the dump by three mongooses finds his way to the sea and regains his powers. He disguises himself as a surfer and follows 'Ula Li'i (Little Red) to her grandmother's house to steal her basket of food. Includes a glossary of Hawaiian and pidgin words used and a pronunciation guide.

209   LOWELL, SUSAN.   *Little Red Cowboy Hat.*

Ill. by Randy Cecil. Henry Holt, 1997

ISBN: 978-0-8050-3508-7

Country/Culture: Western

Motifs: Cowboys

Gender role reversal

Animals (wolves or coyotes)

Little Red has both a red hat and bright red hair. When she goes to Grandma's ranch to deliver homemade bread and cactus jelly, there is a wolf in Grandma's bed. Grandma, who had been out chopping wood, comes in and chases the wolf out with her shotgun. Then Grandma and Little Red sit down for a nice snack of bread and jelly.

210   MERRILL, JEAN. *Red Riding: A Story of How Katy Tells Tony a Story Because It Is Raining.*

Ill. by Ronni Solbert. Pantheon Books, 1968

ISBN: 978-0-394-91534-0

Motifs: Animals (wolves or coyotes)

Two children sit inside on a rainy day and recount the story. As older sister Katy tries to get the story straight, younger brother Tony adds creative embellishments to make it more interesting. They debate exactly what is in Red's basket (deviled eggs, Tony's favorite), and what illness the grandmother has contracted (chicken pox), and discuss the many types of wild animals Red may encounter in the forest, such as hippos and tigers.

211   ROBERTS, LYNN. *Little Red: A Fizzingly Good Yarn.*

Ill. by David Roberts. Harry N. Abrams, 2005

ISBN: 978-0-8109-5783-1

Motifs: Animals (wolves or coyotes)

Gender role reversal

Thomas, whom everybody calls Red, helps his parents run an inn where they make their own ginger ale. One day as he goes through the woods to take some ginger ale to Granny's, the wolf spies him and decides to make a meal of the two of them. He gets to Granny's house, eats her, and waits for Red to appear. When Red gets there, he convinces the wolf that the ginger ale is tastier than himself. The wolf chugs down the ginger ale and produces a burp so large that Granny is saved.

212   ROWLAND, DELLA. *Little Red Riding Hood: The Wolf's Tale.*

Ill. by Michael Montgomery. Carol Pub. Group, 1991

ISBN: 978-1-55972-072-4

Motifs: Animals (wolves or coyotes)

Food

Part of the publisher's Upside Down Tales series. This edition has the original tale in the first part, then readers turn the book over to get the wolf's side of the story. In the version narrated by the wolf, he insists that Red Riding Hood was constantly pestering him to stop stealing chickens and eat healthy food. He was merely hiding from her in Granny's bedroom when he was accused of eating Granny.

213   SWEET, MELISSA.   *Carmine: A Little More Red.*
Houghton Mifflin, 2005
ISBN: 978-0-618-38794-6
Motifs: Food (soup or stew)
           Animals (wolves or coyotes)

Carmine's granny loves to make her alphabet soup, so the story is told alphabetically. Each page or section highlights one letter that starts a word in the story. B is for beware of dangers, which granny told her to do before she left. E is for exquisite, which describes the weather that day, and L is for lurking, which is what the wolf was doing in the woods. Includes a recipe for Granny's Alphabet soup.

214   YOUNG, ED.   *Lon Po Po: A Red-Riding Hood Story from China.*
Philomel Books, 1989
ISBN: 978-0-399-21619-0
Country/Culture: China
Motifs: Animals (wolves or coyotes)
           Food (nuts)

The mother leaves three children alone in the house while she visits grandma. The wolf, seeing that the children have been left alone, knocks on the door and claims to be Po Po, "Grandma." The children let the wolf in, but discover that they have been fooled. Turning the tables on the wolf, the children climb a tree to safety, claiming to get gingko nuts for Po Po.

RUMPELSTILTSKIN

This story is also found in *English Fairy Tales Collected by Joseph Jacobs* (Third edition, revised. G.P. Putnam's Sons, 1902) with the title "Tom Tit Tot." That version begins similarly to Grimms's "The Gallant Tailor" (*Household Stories by the Brothers Grimm* [Macmillan and Company, 1886.]) A mother brags to her king that her daughter had "spun five skeins today" when in truth the girl had eaten five pies. The king offers to marry the girl if she can spin five skeins every night for a month. The creature that appears to the girl is described as a "small little black thing with a long tail" that he spins around in his hand. The creature does her spinning for her, and she agrees to go with him if she can't guess her name. Rather than sending a servant out to find the name as in Grimm, the girl accidentally discovers it from the king. When she tells the name, Tom Tit Tot screams and flies away, but does not self-destruct as in Grimm. The version below is abridged from *Household Stories by the Brothers Grimm*.

THERE WAS A POOR MILLER WHO HAD A BEAUTIFUL DAUGHTER. One day he spoke with the king, and bragged that his daughter could spin straw into gold. The king said to the miller, "If she is as clever as you say, bring her to my castle tomorrow to show me."

The next day the king took her to a room full of straw, gave her a spindle, and said, "Now set to work, and if by the early morning you have not spun this straw into gold, I will have your head." And he shut the door and left her there.

And so the poor miller's daughter was left sitting there, distressed because she had no idea how to do this. As she began to weep, the door opened, and in came a little man who said,

"Good evening, why are you crying?"

"Oh!" answered the girl, "I have to spin gold out of straw, and I don't know how."

Then the little man said,

"What will you give me if I spin it for you?"

"My necklace," said the girl.

The little man took the necklace, seated himself before the wheel, and began to spin. And so he went till morning, until all the bobbins were full of gold. When the king came and saw the gold he was astonished and became greedy. The girl was taken into a much bigger room filled with straw, and again told to spin or lose her life. Once more, the little man appeared.

"What will you give me?" He asked.

"This ring," she answered.

So the little man took the ring, and by the next morning all the straw was spun into glistening gold. The king rejoiced beyond measure at the sight, but he was greedy and could never have enough. He took her to a larger room with the same instructions.

The little man appeared for the third time and said, "What will you give me this time?"

"I have nothing left," she answered.

"Then you must promise me your first child," he said.

"Who knows if that will happen?" she thought, but in her necessity, she swore him this, and he did as he promised. When the king came in the morning and found the gold, he decided to marry her at once.

In a year's time she bore a child, and shortly after the little man returned.

He said, "Now give me what you promised."

The queen was terrified and offered him riches instead, but the little man refused.

The queen cried, and the little man pitied her.

"I will give you three days to guess my name," he said. "But if you cannot, I will have the child."

The queen spent the whole night thinking of names, and sent a messenger out to ask for all the names that could be found. When the little man came the next day she repeated all she knew, but after each the little man said, "That is not my name."

The second day was like the first. She could not guess his name.

The third day the messenger came back and said,

"As I came to a high hill, atop it was a fire, and round the fire danced a comical little man, hopping on one leg, singing,

"To-day do I bake, to-morrow I brew,
The day after that the queen's child comes in;
And oh! I am glad that nobody knew
That the name I am called is Rumpelstiltskin!"

The queen was very pleased. When the little man came and said, "Now, Mrs. Queen, what is my name?" she said at first,

"Is it Jack?"

"No," he answered.

"Harry?"

"No," he answered.

"Then perhaps your name is Rumpelstiltskin!" she cried.

"The devil told you that!" cried the little man, and he stamped his right foot so hard that it went into the ground. Then with both his hands he seized his left foot in such a fury that he split in two, and that was the end of him.

—◆—

215 CRUMP, FRED H. *Rumpelstiltskin.*
Winston-Derek Publishers, 1992
ISBN: 978-1-55523-409-6
Country/Culture: African American
Motifs: Monsters, beasts, or magical creatures
This version stays close to the original, with the addition of African American characters in the illustrations. Glinda is the miller's daughter who must contract with Rumpelstiltskin to spin gold from straw. Along with the text, each illustration is accompanied by a banner describing the scene depicted.

216 GRANOWSKY, ALVIN. *A Deal Is a Deal!*
Ill. by Linda Dockey Graves. Steck-Vaughn, 1993
ISBN: 978-0-8114-2213-0
Motifs: Monsters, beasts, or magical creatures
Part of the publisher's Point of View series, this edition tells the original tale in the first part, and then the book is turned over to read Rumpelstiltskin's story. In the version narrated by Rumpelstiltskin, he is being nice by helping the miller's daughter spin straw into gold. When he goes to collect on her promise of a child, the queen sends her army out to invade his privacy like paparazzi in order to find out his name.

217 HAMILTON, VIRGINIA. *The Girl Who Spun Gold.*
Ill. by Leo Dillon. Blue Sky Press, 2000
ISBN: 978-0-590-47378-1
Country/Culture: Caribbean
Motifs: Monsters, beasts, or magical creatures
In this West Indian version, Quashiba is married to the king for one year before he begins to make demands on her to spin gold from cotton. After she rids herself of Litmahn Bittyun, the tiny, ugly magical man who helped her spin the cotton into gold, she continues to be married to the king but refuses to speak to him for three years.

218 MOSER, BARRY. *Tucker Pfeffercorn: An Old Story Retold.*
Little, Brown, 1994
ISBN: 978-0-316-58542-2
Country/Culture: Appalachia
Motifs: Monsters, beasts, or magical creatures

A mountain version of the story in which the king is the local robber baron who locks Bessie Grace in a shed to spin the gold. When her captor mysteriously dies, the "peculiar little man" who helped her with the spinning shows up at her home to claim his prize.

219   STANLEY, DIANE. *Rumpelstiltskin's Daughter.*
Morrow Junior Books, 1997
ISBN: 978-0-688-14327-5
Motifs: Monsters, beasts, or magical creatures
Rumpelstiltskin and the miller's daughter run off together and have a child who, strangely enough, runs into some problems very similar to her mother's when she grows up. Being a liberated young woman, though, she manages to outsmart the king by convincing him to give away his gold. In the end he offers to marry her, but she chooses to become the prime minister instead.

220   STEWIG, JOHN W. *Whuppity Stoorie.*
Ill. by Preston McDaniels. Holiday House, 2004
ISBN: 978-0-8234-1749-0
Country/Culture: Scotland
Motifs: Animals (pigs)
         Monsters, beasts, or magical creatures
A farm wife makes a deal with a strange woman. In order to save her pig from death, the wife agrees to give the woman her son. The pig is saved, but when the woman demands the farm wife's son, the mother refuses. In order to keep the strange woman from taking her child, the mother is given three opportunities to guess her name, which she finds out is Whuppity Stoorie. When she hears the mother say her name, the witch flies into a rage and dissolves into a puff of smoke.

221   WHITE, CAROLYN. *Whuppity Stoorie: A Scottish Folktale.*
Ill. by S. D. Schindler. Putnam, 1997
ISBN: 978-0-399-22903-9
Country/Culture: Scotland
Motifs: Animals (pigs)
         Monsters, beasts, or magical creatures
In order to save her dying pig, a Scottish farm wife agrees to give a mysterious fairy in a green hood anything she asks for. The fairy cures the pig and demands the farm wife's Kate. To keep the fairy from taking her child, the wife is given three opportunities to guess her name, which is Whuppity Stoorie.

222   ZEMACH, HARVE.   *Duffy and the Devil.*

Ill. by Margot Zemach. Farrar, Straus and Giroux, 1973

ISBN: 978-0-374-31887-1

Motifs: Clothing

Monsters, beasts, or magical creatures

Duffy tells the squire that she can "spin like a saint," but when she actually has to do it, she promises the devil that she will go away with him in three years if he does all the spinning. Duffy manages to find out the devil's name, but when he hears it he disappears in a puff of smoke, and so does all the clothing that he made, including those the squire is wearing.

THE SHOEMAKER AND THE ELVES

Abridged from *Household Stories by the Brothers Grimm* (Macmillan and Company, 1886).

THERE WAS ONCE A SHOEMAKER WHO WAS SO POOR that all he had left was enough leather to make one pair of shoes. He cut out the shoes at night, so as to work on them the next morning, and went to bed and fell asleep. In the morning he found the pair of shoes made and finished, standing on his table. He was very much astonished, and did not know what to think. He picked them up and found that every stitch was in its right place, as if the shoes had come from a master workman.

Soon after, a customer entered and the shoes fit him perfectly, so he paid more than the usual price for them. The shoemaker now had enough money to buy leather for two more pairs of shoes. He cut them out that night, intending to set to work on them the next morning. But again when he awoke they were already finished. And a customer came who gave him so much money that the shoemaker was able to buy leather for four new pairs. Early next morning he found the four pairs also finished, and so it continued; whatever he cut out in the evening was worked up by the morning.

One night before Christmas, when the shoemaker had finished cutting out the leather he said to his wife,

"Why don't we sit up tonight and see who does this for us?"

His wife agreed and they both hid in a corner of the room to watch. At midnight in came two naked little men who set to work. They stitched and hammered so cleverly and quickly that the shoemaker was amazed. They kept working until everything was finished and then they ran off.

The next morning the wife said to her husband, "Those little men have made us rich, and we should be grateful. With all their running about with no clothes, they must be very cold. I will make clothing for them, and knit them stockings, and you can make each a pair of shoes."

The shoemaker agreed, and when everything was finished, they laid the gifts together on the table, instead of the cut-out work. When midnight came, the little men rushed in, ready to set to work. When they found the neat little garments set out for them, they stood a moment in surprise and then squealed in delight. With the greatest swiftness they slipped them on, singing,

"What spruce and dandy boys are we!
No longer cobblers we will be."

Then they hopped and danced about, jumping over the chairs and tables, and danced out the door and were never seen again.

223   LAURENCE, JIM, AND TIM HILDEBRANDT.   *The Shoemaker and the Christmas Elves.*

Ill. by Tim Hildebrandt. Derrydale Books, 1993
ISBN: 978-0-517-08488-5

Motifs: Clothing (shoes or boots)
            Holidays (Christmas)

This version is similar to the original tale, but links the magical shoe-making elves to Santa Claus's workshop. The story starts with Santa sending a few of his elves out on a special errand. When the elves are discovered by the shoemaker, he decides to make them clothes as Christmas presents. The elves receive their gifts on Christmas Eve and run outside to meet up with Santa, who is waiting outside for them with his sleigh full of toys.

224   LOWELL, SUSAN.   *The Bootmaker and the Elves.*

Ill. by Tom Curry. Orchard Books, 1997
ISBN: 978-0-531-30044-2

Country/Culture: Western

Motifs: Clothing (shoes or boots)

Told in a Western setting and a cowboy dialect, this story stays close to the original. The shoes the elves make for the bootmaker are tall, shiny, and black as midnight cowboy boots, hand-tooled with stars, roses, and horseshoes for good luck.

225   ROGERS, FRED.   *The Elves, the Shoemaker, and the Shoemaker's Wife : A Retold Tale.*
Ill. by Richard Hefter. Small World Enterprises, 1973
ISBN: 978-0-88460-002-2
Motifs: Clothing (shoes or boots)

Set in a contemporary town, the plot follows the original tale. The elves already have clothing and the shoemaker's wife has a job making television commercials. In the end, the elves choose to live with the shoemaker and his wife instead of running away.

SLEEPING BEAUTY

Abridged from *Household Stories by the Brothers Grimm* (Macmillan and Company, 1886).

ONCE THERE WERE A KING AND QUEEN WHO WISHED for a child but had none. One day as the queen was bathing a frog appeared and said to her,

"Before a year has gone by you will have your wish and bring a daughter into the world."

And so it happened. The queen bore a daughter and the king ordained a great feast. Everyone was invited, including the wise women, who might find favor with the child. There were thirteen, but he had only twelve golden plates so one of them had to be left out. As the feast drew to a close, the wise women came to give the child their gifts of virtue, beauty, and so on. When eleven had said their say, in came the uninvited thirteenth, set on revenge. She cried,

"In her fifteenth year the princess shall prick herself with a spindle and die!"

That said, she left the hall. Everyone was terrified, so the twelfth woman came forward, and though she could not reverse the prophecy, she could soften it, so she said,

"The princess shall not die, but fall into a deep sleep."

But the king, trying to avoid even this, ordered all the spindles in the castle destroyed.

So the girl grew up, adorned with the gifts of the wise women; and everyone loved her.

When the princess was fifteen, the king and queen rode abroad, and left her alone in the castle. She wandered all about till at last she came to an old tower. She climbed the stairs and opened the door at the top, and found an old woman with a spindle, diligently spinning.

"Good day," said the princess, "what are you doing?"

"I am spinning," answered the old woman.

"What is that?" asked the maiden. She reached out, but no sooner had she touched the spindle than the prophecy was fulfilled. She fell upon the bed asleep. This sleep fell upon the whole court and castle. The king and queen, who had entered the great hall, fell fast asleep, as did all the animals. And the wind ceased, and not a leaf fell from the trees. Finally, a hedge of thorns grew around the castle, until at last it was hidden from view.

After many years a prince came to that country. He heard an old man speak of the legend of Rosamond the enchanted princess who had slept with her court for a hundred years behind the great hedge. The old man warned the prince of many others who had died trying to get through the hedge, but the prince said, "I am not afraid. I will find the lovely Rosamond."

Now the hundred years were at an end, and the day had come when Rosamond should be awakened. When the prince drew near the hedge, it changed into beautiful large flowers that parted to let him pass. When he reached the castle-yard, he saw the people and the animals lying asleep, but he continued on. Then he went into the hall and saw the court lying asleep, and above them, the king and the queen. And still he went on, until at last he came to the tower, climbed the winding stair, and opened the door to the room where Rosamond lay. When he saw her looking so lovely in her sleep, he could not turn away. He stooped and kissed her, and she awakened. She rose, and they went forth together, and everyone woke up, the animals and the court and the king and queen, and gazed around with eyes of wonderment.

And so it was that the wedding of the prince and Rosamond was held with great splendor, and they lived happily ever after.

226   CRADDOCK, SONIA. *Sleeping Boy.*

Ill. by Leonid Gore. Atheneum, 1999

ISBN: 978-0-689-81763-2

Country/Culture: Germany

Motifs: Music (big band)

In prewar Germany, Knabe Rosen and his family are cursed to fall asleep when they hear a marching band on Knabe's sixteenth birthday. The counter-curse allows them to sleep through World War II and the rise of the USSR. They are awakened by the sound of the Berlin Wall being torn down outside their window.

SLEEPING BEAUTY   121

227   KELLAR, EMILY.   *Sleeping Bunny.*
Ill. by Pamela Silin-Palmer. Random House, 2003
ISBN: 978-0-375-81541-6
Motifs: Animals (rabbits or hares)
        Animals (mice or rats)

Illustrated with elaborate and detailed oil paintings, this is a standard retelling of the story. The main characters are rabbits and the fairies are monarch-winged pigs. On Princess Bunny's fifteenth birthday, the king and queen throw a party to celebrate, and the princess wanders off and meets a green rat witch who is spinning thread in a remote tower in the castle.

228   LASKY, KATHRYN.   *Humphrey, Albert, and the Flying Machine.*
Ill. by John Manders. Harcourt, 2004
ISBN: 978-0-15-216235-1
Motifs: Transportation (airplanes)

Briar Rose's party is so boring that everyone falls asleep, including two brothers Humphrey and Albert. They awaken after a hundred years, but neither wants to kiss Briar Rose (kissing? gross!) to wake everyone else up. So they go on a hunt for a mate for Rose and meet up with Daniel Bernoulli, an inventor who is never boring. He kisses Briar Rose and they are never bored again.

229   MAYER, MERCER.   *The Sleeping Beauty.*
Atheneum, 1994
ISBN: 978-0-02-765340-3
Motifs: Birds (owls)

The Blue Fairy curses the king and queen because she was served from a lead goblet. The curse is modified by the Star Fairy to include the appearance of a silver owl. The owl appears and the queen has a child, but the Blue Fairy again curses them. The child will die when pricked by a needle. Again the Star Fairy intervenes, and changes the curse to only make her sleep. The story follows the original after this. Initially published in 1984.

230   MINTERS, FRANCES.   *Sleepless Beauty.*
Ill. by G. Brian Karas. Viking, 1996
ISBN: 978-0-670-87033-2

Motifs: Music

This version of the story is set in a modern city and told in rhyme. Sleepless Beauty pricks her finger on an old-fashioned record needle. This puts her to sleep, but instead of napping for a hundred years, she awakens the next morning because she was smart enough to set her alarm.

231   OSBORNE, WILL, AND MARY POPE OSBORNE.   *Sleeping Bobby.*

Ill. by Giselle Potter. Atheneum, 2005
ISBN: 978-0-689-87668-4
Motifs: Gender role reversal

In this story, the child who is cursed by the fairy and sleeps for one hundred years is a boy. The woman who curses him to die at his party is one of the kingdom's Wise Women. She was left out of the celebration because the queen didn't have enough place settings for all of them at the table.

SNOW WHITE

Adapted from *Household Stories by the Brothers Grimm* (Macmillan and Company, 1886).

ONCE THERE WAS A QUEEN WHO WISHED DESPERATELY for a child. "Oh that I had a child as white as snow, as red as blood, and as black as the wood of this frame!" she prayed.

Shortly she had such a daughter, and named her Snow-white, but the queen died that very day.

After a year the king married a beautiful woman who was so vain she could not bear to be surpassed in beauty by any one. She had a magic looking-glass, and she would look in it and say,

"Looking-glass upon the wall,

Who is fairest of us all?"

And the looking-glass would answer,

"You are fairest of them all."

And she was content, because she knew it was the truth.

Now, when Snow-white was seven years old she was as beautiful as day. So when the queen went to her mirror and said,

"Looking-glass upon the wall,

Who is fairest of us all?"

It answered,

"Queen, you are beautiful, 'tis true,

But Snow-white fairer is than you."

The queen was shocked, and she became green with envy, and hated Snow-white. She sent for a huntsman, and said,

"Take Snow-white into the woods. Put her to death, and bring me her heart to eat."

The huntsman consented, and led her away; but in the woods, Snow-white began to weep, and said,

"Please do not kill me. Let me run away, and I will never return."

The huntsman had pity on her and said, "Run, child."

On his return, the hunter killed a wild boar and took out the heart. Then he presented it to the queen and she ate it.

When the hunter freed her, Snow-white ran through the woods until she came to an empty house. There she let herself in and collapsed on a bed, sound asleep.

The masters of the house were seven dwarfs who were miners. When they came home, they found Snow-white asleep in the house.

The dwarfs said, "If you will keep house for us, you may stay."

And so she stayed. Every morning the dwarfs went out, and all day the girl was left alone. So the good little dwarfs warned her, saying,

"Beware your step-mother. Let no one in."

The queen believed Snow-white was dead, and so she went to her mirror, and said,

"Looking-glass upon the wall,

Who's fairest of us all?"

And the glass answered,

"Queen, thou art of beauty rare,

But Snow-white living in the glen

Is a thousand times more fair."

So she was furious the huntsman had deceived her. She dressed herself as an old apple peddler and went to the house in the glen. She knocked at the door and cried, "Apples for sale! Will you buy my apples?"

Snow-white answered, "I cannot let anyone in."

"All right," answered the woman; "I can sell my apples elsewhere. Here, I will give you one."

"No," answered Snow-white. "I dare not take anything."

"Don't be afraid," said the woman, "look, we will share the apple."

Snow-white longed for the beautiful apple. She stretched out her hand and took the half which was poisoned. As soon as she bit, Snow-white fell to the earth as dead.

The queen went home and asked the looking-glass,

"Looking-glass against the wall,

Who is fairest of us all?"

It answered, "You are the fairest of all."

Then her envious heart had peace, as much as an envious heart can have.

When the dwarfs came home they found Snow-white lying on the ground, as if dead. They said,

"We cannot put her in the ground." They made a coffin of glass, and they laid her in it, and wrote on it her name, and that she was a princess. So she lay for many years, never changing.

One day a king's son rode up to the dwarfs' house. He saw the coffin, and beautiful Snow-white. He said to the dwarfs,

"Please give me the coffin. I cannot live without Snow-white. She is my heart's desire."

So the dwarfs pitied him and consented. His servants carried the coffin away, but as they went they stumbled over a bush and shook the bit of poisoned apple out of her throat. Snow-white opened her eyes and sat up, alive and well.

"Where am I?" cried she. The king's son joyfully answered, "You are near me," and told all that had happened.

"You are my heart's desire. Come to my father's castle and be my bride." So Snow-white agreed, and a great feast was planned to celebrate the marriage.

The wicked step-mother was bidden to the feast, but when she saw Snow-white she could not contain her anger and terror. So the prince prepared red-hot iron shoes, and the wicked stepmother had to dance in them until she fell down dead.

232   COLLINS, SHEILA HÉBERT.   *Blanchette et les Sept Petits Cajuns: A Cajun Snow White.*
Ill. by Patrick Soper. Pelican, 2002
ISBN: 978-1-56554-912-8
Country/Culture: Cajun
Motifs: Animals (alligators or crocodiles)
    Food (soup or stew)
    Monsters, beasts, or magical creatures

Marie Gaudet practices voodoo in the Honey Island Swamp. Every day she asks the foggy bayou who is the fairest of all, and the bayou replies that she is. When Blanchette becomes the most beautiful, Marie lures her into the swamp so she will get lost, but instead Blanchette finds a hut belonging to seven small Cajun men. Includes pronunciation guide and definitions for French words on each page. Also has a recipe for chicken and sausage jambalaya.

233   DELESSERT, ETIENNE.   *The Seven Dwarfs: As Told to Etienne Delessert by Stephane, the Duke of the Forest in the Autumn of 1613.*
Creative Editions, 2001
ISBN: 978-1-56846-139-7
Motifs: Monsters, beasts, or magical creatures

After the seven dwarfs help save Snow White, the king invites them to live at the castle as a reward. They live in the kingdom as honored gentlemen for some time, but aren't as happy as they thought they would be. They finally realize that they were more comfortable being humble miners and that they belong in the forest.

234   FRENCH, FIONA.   *Snow White in New York.*
Oxford University Press, 1986
ISBN: 978-0-19-279808-4
Motifs: Music (jazz)
Told as a Jazz Age story. Snow White is the belle of New York City. When her stepmother throws her out of the house, Snow White joins a band of seven jazz musicians. Her prince is a handsome reporter who is certain of Snow White's talent as a jazz singer.

235   GRANOWSKY, ALVIN.   *The Unfairest of Them All.*
Ill. by Mike Krone. Steck-Vaughn, 1993
ISBN: 978-0-8114-2201-7
Motifs: Fruits and vegetables (apples)
This title is part of the publisher's Point of View series. This version has the original tale in the first part, and then the book is turned over to read the stepmother's story. In the story narrated by the stepmother, Snow White is a vain and vindictive girl determined to break up her marriage to Snow White's father.

236   HELLER, CATHERINE.   *Snow White: The Untold Story.*
Ill. by Karen Stolper. Carol Pub. Group, 1995
ISBN: 978-1-55972-326-8
Motifs: Fruits and vegetables (apples)
According to the stepmother, Blanche is a spoiled young lady obsessed with beauty. Blanche discovers the cottage of seven little men and decides to stay. Her stepmother tries to rescue her by giving her an apple filled with a sleeping potion, but the seven men put her in a glass coffin and charge admission.

237   KIMMEL, ERIC A.   *Rimonah of the Flashing Sword: A North African Tale.*
Ill. by Omar Rayyan. Holiday House, 1995
ISBN: 978-0-8234-1093-4
Country/Culture: Africa
Motifs: Monsters, beasts, or magical creatures
Rimonah's stepmother uses a porcelain bowl to tell her she is the most beautiful woman in the land. When the bowl tells her Rimonah is the most beautiful, Rimonah is taken into the forest to be killed. The girl escapes and joins a band of forty thieves and becomes Rimonah of the Flashing Sword. When she returns to the kingdom to reclaim her place, the stepmother flies off on a magic carpet. Rimonah shatters the magic bowl,

destroying the flying carpet and killing the stepmother. Includes author's note on the origin of the tale and illustrator's note on the graphic influences in the illustrations.

238 LAIRD, DONIVEE MARTIN. *Hau Kea and the Seven Menehune.*

Ill. by Carol Ann Jossem. Barnaby Books, 1995
ISBN: 978-0-940350-26-7
Country/Culture: Hawaii
Motifs: Fruits and vegetables
          Monsters, beasts, or magical creatures

The seven Menehune brothers shelter Hau Kea, a young village girl whom the queen of O'ahu has sworn to destroy because of her superior beauty. The queen tries to kill the girl by giving her a poison guava, but Hau Kea only falls asleep and the Menehune brothers put her to bed in their hut. The king of Kaua'i discovers her on a walk through the woods and kisses her to wake her up, but it isn't until all seven Menehune brothers also kiss her that she awakens. Includes a glossary of Hawaiian and pidgin words used and a pronunciation guide.

239 THALER, MIKE. *Schmoe White and the Seven Dorfs.*

Ill. by Jared D. Lee. Scholastic, 1997
ISBN: 978-0-590-89824-9
Motifs: Music

Schmoe White finds the band "The Seven Dorfs" — Nerdy, Grouchy, Funky, Smiley, Drowsy, Wheezy, and Hip — practicing in their cabin. She becomes the lead singer, and they play gigs all over the forest. Wicked Queen tracks her down and poisons her with Pass-Out Pink lipstick. Prince happens to walk by and saves her with a kiss, but then he gets the lipstick on himself and lapses into unconsciousness. They go back and forth with this until the Dorfs get bored and start a baseball team. Part of the Happily Ever Laughter series.

STONE SOUP

Variations of this story involve an army entering a town where the residents claim all their food was stolen by the retreating army. And the lead officer induces the residents to share in their stone soup. The main ingredient is usually a rock or a nail, but other inanimate objects can be used. The version below is "The Old Woman and the Tramp," adapted from *Scandinavian Folk and Fairy Tales,* edited by Claire Booss.

ONE EVENING, A TRAMP CAME TO A SMALL HOUSE. He knocked on the door and an old woman answered. "Please, ma'am, may I have a place to sleep and a bite to eat?" he inquired.

"This is not an inn!" she replied. "You may sleep by the hearth, but I haven't any food. I haven't had a bite myself all day."

"Well, better a warm hearth than the cold dirt," thought the tramp and he followed her inside. "My good lady, if you haven't eaten today, you must be ravenous," he said to her. "Would you like a share of mine?"

"What on earth could you give me?" she inquired, because he looked as if he had nothing more than the clothes on his back.

"Oh, I have traveled many places," he replied, "and have learned how to make nail soup. Will you lend me your pot?"

The old woman was curious, so she handed him the pot. He filled it with water and set it on the fire. Then he reached in his pocket and retrieved an old, rusted nail. This he threw into the water.

"That's it?" asked the woman.

"Well, it tastes much better with salt, but since we have none, this will have to do."

"I can probably find a bit of that," she said. So she went to her pantry and made some noise and came out with a handful of salt, which she threw into the pot.

The tramp thanked her and continued to stir.

"So that's it?" the woman asked again.

"It would taste heavenly with some salted pork," the tramp replied, "but since we have none, this will suffice."

"Let me look to see if there is some I have overlooked," said the old woman, and she went back to the larder. She clattered around a bit, and came forth with the meat.

"I found this. Do you think it will help?" she asked the tramp.

"That should do nicely," he said as he put it in the pot.

"So now, that is all you do?" she asked once more. "How will that taste?"

"To be honest, I made it once for the Queen," said the tramp, "and it was just delicious. But we had potatoes to put in it. This will have to do for us now."

Well, the old woman had never eaten the same food as a queen, and was interested to taste such grand fare, so she went back to her pantry and brought forth two potatoes.

"Lucky us! Look what I found!" she said. And she peeled and chopped the potatoes, and put them in the water.

Now the old woman was keen to eat just like the Queen, and she went to her cupboard and took down a flask of brandy and two crystal goblets, butter and a loaf of bread, and a length of sausage. The table was now set with a feast, and when the tramp declared the soup ready, they ate and drank and had themselves a grand time. "And to think," thought the old lady, "all of this came from just one nail!"

After a bit, they decided to retire, and the tramp took his place by the hearth. But the old woman would not hear of it. "Come use my trundle," she insisted. "The floor is no place for such a grand man as you."

After a good night's sleep, the old woman woke her guest with coffee and breakfast. Then she placed a coin in his hand and said, "Never has there been a finer gentleman. Now I will never be impoverished, for I will always be able to make nail soup!" And as he tramped away, she thought, "What an extraordinary person!"

---

240   BONNING, TONY. *Fox Tale Soup.*

Ill. by Sally Hobson. Simon & Schuster, 2002

ISBN: 978-0-689-84900-8

Motifs: Cooking

Food (soup or stew)

Animals

Animals (foxes)

A clever fox is traveling the countryside and stops at a farm to ask for food. All the animals claim they have nothing extra to share, so the fox starts boiling a pot of water with a rock in it. Eventually the fox is able to convince each of the animals in the barnyard to contribute a little to his soup so that they can all share.

241   BRENNER, BARBARA.   *Group Soup: A Bank Street Book About Values.*

Ill. by Lynn Munsinger. Viking, 1992
ISBN: 978-0-670-82867-8
Motifs: Cooking
    Food (soup or stew)

Mama Bunny has to take care of Grandma and doesn't have time to make dinner. Her six little bunnies have to learn to work together to make a whole meal for everyone. Each bunny contributes a vegetable that they have stored away until a fine soup is made.

242   COMPESTINE, YING CHANG.   *The Real Story of Stone Soup.*

Ill. by Stephane Jorisch. Dutton Children's Books, 2007
ISBN: 978-0-525-47493-7
Motifs: Cooking
    Food (soup or stew)

Narrated by a Chinese uncle who insists that his is the real recipe for stone soup. He tells how he convinces his three lazy nephews to make soup out of nothing and how they become more industrious because of it. The illustrations show how the nephews dupe the uncle instead. Includes author's note on the origin of the story and a recipe for egg drop stone soup.

243   DAVIS, AUBREY.   *Bone Button Borscht.*

Ill. by Dusan Petricic. Kids Can Press, 1997
ISBN: 978-1-55074-224-4
Country/Culture: Jewish
Motifs: Cooking
    Food (soup or stew)

A beggar enters a town where there is no sign of life. He knocks on doors, but everyone refuses to help him. He enters the synagogue looking for food, but even the caretaker there refuses him. Finally, the beggar starts to make a stew out of his coat buttons, thereby arousing the curiosity of all the villagers. He is able to convince everyone that his buttons made of bone can make a magic soup, if everyone contributes just a bit.

244   GERSHATOR, DAVID, AND PHILLIS GERSHATOR.   *Kallaloo! A Caribbean Tale.*

Ill. by Diane Greenseid. Marshall Cavendish, 2005
ISBN: 978-0-7614-5110-5
Country/Culture: Caribbean
Motifs: Cooking
         Food (soup or stew)

Granny is so hungry her belly is bawling, but she doesn't have any food or money with which to buy it. She finds a magic conch shell and takes it to the market square and promises to make everyone some kallaloo with it. Slowly the stew is made as each of the sellers contributes a bit to the pot. Includes author's note on Caribbean culture, and a recipe for kallaloo.

245   KIMMEL, ERIC.   *Cactus Soup.*

Ill. by Paul Huling. Marshall Cavendish, 2004
ISBN: 978-0-7614-5155-6
Country/Culture: Mexico
Motifs: Cooking
         Food (soup or stew)

The citizens of San Miguel spy a troop of soldiers entering their town. Believing that the soldiers will decimate their food supply, the citizens decide to hide their food and tell the soldiers they have nothing to share. When the captain learns of the town's suspicious misfortune, he cleverly agrees to make a huge pot of cactus soup for everyone. After dropping a cactus thorn into a pot of boiling water and tasting it, the captain comments that cactus soup always tastes better with salt. The townspeople, in an effort to see how cactus soup is made, eventually provide the captain with every ingredient needed to make his soup and a memorable fiesta. The townspeople learn that by working together, they can feed an entire army and no longer need to be selfish.

246   MUTH, JON J.   *Stone Soup.*

Scholastic, 2003
ISBN: 978-0-439-33909-4
Country/Culture: China
Motifs: Cooking
         Food (soup or stew)

Three monks — Hok, Lok, and Siew — are nomads who meditate on what makes people happy. One day they come to a village where the people have grown very distrusting of each other. The three monks are able to make the villagers into a community again by convincing them to individually contribute what they can to the empty soup pot.

247   PATRON, SUSAN.   *Burgoo Stew.*
Ill. by Mike Shenon. Orchard Books, 1991
ISBN: 978-0-531-05916-6
Motifs: Cooking
        Food (soup or stew)

Five mean and ornery boys go to old Billy Que and demand something to eat. Billy convinces each to go home and bring back one ingredient so that he can make his burgoo stew, and in the process teaches the boys about compassion and cooperation.

248   ROSS, TONY.   *Stone Soup.*
Dial Books for Young Readers, 1987
ISBN: 978-0-8037-0118-2
Motifs: Cooking
        Food (soup or stew)
        Animals (wolves or coyotes)
        Birds (chickens)

Big Bad Wolf goes to Little Red Hen's house and declares that he is going to eat her. She convinces him to have a bowl of her homemade stone soup first, and gets him to clean her house while he is waiting. When the wolf has finished the soup, he is too full and tired to eat the hen, but steals the stone as he leaves.

249   STEWIG, JOHN W.   *Stone Soup.*
Ill. by Margot Tomes. Holiday House, 1991
ISBN: 978-0-8234-0863-4
Motifs: Cooking
        Food (soup or stew)
        Gender role reversal

Very similar to the original story, but it is a girl who must leave home to look for food to keep her family from starving. When she gets to the village she convinces the occupants to contribute to a community pot of soup. In the end Grethel returns home with plenty to share with her family.

THE THREE BILLY GOATS GRUFF

As published in *Popular Tales from the Norse* by George Dasent (Third ed. David Douglas, 1888).

ONCE ON A TIME THERE WERE THREE BILLY-GOATS, who were to go up to the hill-side to make themselves fat, and the name of all three was "Gruff."

On the way up was a bridge over a burn they had to cross; and under the bridge lived a great ugly Troll, with eyes as big as saucers, and a nose as long as a poker.

So first of all came the youngest billy-goat Gruff to cross the bridge.

"Trip, trap; trip, trap!" went the bridge.

"WHO"S THAT tripping over my bridge?" roared the Troll.

"Oh! it is only I, the tiniest billy-goat Gruff; and I"m going up to the hill-side to make myself fat," said the billy-goat, with such a small voice.

"Now, I"m coming to gobble you up," said the Troll.

"Oh, no! pray don"t take me. I"m too little, that I am," said the billy-goat; "wait a bit till the second billy-goat Gruff comes, he"s much bigger."

"Well! be off with you," said the Troll.

A little while after came the second billy-goat Gruff to cross the bridge.

"TRIP, TRAP! TRIP, TRAP! TRIP, TRAP!" went the bridge.

"WHO"S THAT tripping over my bridge?" roared the Troll.

"Oh! it"s the second billy-goat Gruff, and I"m going up to the hill-side to make myself fat" said the billy-goat, who hadn"t such a small voice.

"Now, I"m coming to gobble you up," said the Troll.

"Oh, no! don"t take me, wait a little till the big billy-goat Gruff comes, he's much bigger."

"Very well! be off with you," said the Troll.

But just then up came the big billy-goat Gruff.

"TRIP, TRAP! TRIP, TRAP! TRIP, TRAP!" went the bridge, for the billy-goat was so heavy that the bridge creaked and groaned under him.

"WHO"S THAT tramping over my bridge?" roared the Troll.

"IT"S I! THE BIG BILLY-GOAT GRUFF," said the billy-goat, who had an ugly hoarse voice of his own.

"Now, I"m coming to gobble you up," roared the Troll.

"Well, come along! I"ve got two spears,

And I"ll poke your eyeballs out at your ears;

I"ve got besides two curling-stones,

And I"ll crush you to bits, body and bones."

That was what the big billy-goat said; and so he flew at the Troll and poked his eyes out with his horns, and crushed him to bits, body and bones, and tossed him out into the burn, and after that he went up to the hill-side. There the billy-goats got so fat they were scarce able to walk home again; and if the fat hasn't fallen off them, why they're still fat; and so:

Snip, snap, snout,

This tale's told out.

---

250   AARDEMA, VERNA.   _Borreguita and the Coyote: A Tale from Ayutla, Mexico._

Ill. by Petra Mathers. Knopf, 1991

ISBN: 978-0-679-80921-0

Country/Culture: Mexico

Motifs: Animals (wolves or coyotes)

Animals (sheep)

A lamb feeding in a pasture must outsmart the wolf who has come to eat her. She convinces him that the reflection of the moon in the pond is cheese, and he falls in and gets wet. Then she convinces him to hold up a mountain while she runs away. Finally the lamb agrees to jump into his mouth whole, but instead butts him in the head and sends him rolling. Includes glossary of Mexican terms.

251   GRANOWSKY, ALVIN.   _Just a Friendly Old Troll._

Ill. by Michele Nidenoff. Steck-Vaughn, 1996

ISBN: 978-0-8114-7128-2

Motifs: Monsters, beasts, or magical creatures
Animals (goats)

This is part of the author's differing-viewpoint series. The book has the traditional tale on one side, and the retelling on the other. In this version, the troll insists that the goats simply misunderstood his invitation to dinner. He insists that he was actually inviting them to stay for a meal when they thought he was threatening to eat them.

252   HASSETT, JOHN, AND ANN HASSETT.   *Three Silly Girls Grubb.*

Houghton Mifflin, 2002
ISBN: 978-0-618-14183-8
Motifs: School
Food (breads or grains)
Gender role reversal

The three sisters Grubb miss the school bus and must walk across a bridge to school. Ugly-Boy Bobby hides under the bridge and demands ransom from each as they pass. The first two convince him that the next has more jelly donuts than herself. The third threatens to kiss Ugly-Boy Bobby and he decides to behave.

253   PALATINI, MARGIE.   *The Three Silly Billies.*

Ill. by Barry Moser. Simon & Schuster, 2005
ISBN: 978-0-689-85862-8
Motifs: Animals (bears)
Animals (goats)
Monsters, beasts, or magical creatures
Transportation (boats or ships)

Three billy goats come to a troll bridge but don't have enough money to pay the troll toll. They decide to wait and form a car pool with other travelers. The three bears come and get in the pool, followed by Little Red Riding Hood and Jack. Finally with enough riders in the wading pool, they pull the plug and the whoosh of water blows the troll off the bridge.

254   YOUNGQUIST, CATHRENE VALENTE.   *The Three Billygoats Gruff and Mean Calypso Joe.*

Ill. by Kristin Sorra. Atheneum, 2002
ISBN: 978-0-689-82824-9
Country/Culture: Caribbean
Motifs: Monsters, beasts, or magical creatures
Animals (goats)

Calypso Joe is the troll who guards the bridge between two Caribbean islands. The Gruff boys decide they want to eat the greens on the other island. As each goat crosses the bridge, he tells Calypso Joe that the next goat is bigger and meatier. When the third Gruff crosses the bridge, he throws Calypso Joe into the sea.

THE THREE LITTLE PIGS

Abridged from *English Fairy Tales Collected by Joseph Jacobs* (Third edition, revised. G.P. Putnam's Sons, 1902)

STORY OF THE THREE LITTLE PIGS

THERE WAS AN OLD SOW WITH THREE LITTLE PIGS and she sent them out to seek their fortune. The first that went off met a man with a bundle of straw, and said to him:

"Please, man, give me that straw to build a house."

Which the man did, and the little pig built a house with it. Along came a wolf, and knocked at the door, and said:

"Little pig, little pig, let me come in."

The pig answered:

"No, no, by the hair of my chinny chin chin."

The wolf then answered to that:

"Then I'll huff, and I'll puff, and I'll blow your house in."

So he huffed, and he puffed, and he blew his house in, and ate up the little pig.

The second little pig met a man with a bundle of furze [flowers], and said:

"Please, man, give me that furze to build a house."

Which the man did, and the pig built his house. Along came the wolf, and said:

"Little pig, little pig, let me come in."

"No, no, by the hair of my chinny chin chin."

"Then I'll puff, and I'll huff, and I'll blow your house in."

So he huffed, and he puffed, and he puffed, and he huffed, and blew the house down, and he ate up the little pig.

The third little pig met a man with a load of bricks, and said:

"Please, man, give me those bricks to build a house."

So the man gave him the bricks, and he built his house. The wolf came, as he did to the other little pigs, and said:

"Little pig, little pig, let me come in."

"No, no, by the hair of my chinny chin chin."

"Then I'll huff, and I'll puff, and I'll blow your house in."

Well, he huffed, and he puffed, and he huffed and he puffed, and he puffed and huffed; but he could *not* get the house down. When he found that he could not blow the house down, he said:

"Little pig, I know where there is a nice field of turnips."

"Where?" said the little pig.

"Oh, in Mr. Smith's field, and if you will be ready tomorrow morning I will call for you, and we will go together, and get some for dinner."

"Very well," said the little pig, "I will be ready. What time do you mean to go?"

"Oh, at six o'clock."

Well, the little pig got up at five and got the turnips before the wolf came (which he did about six) and said:

"Little Pig, are you ready?"

The little pig said: "Ready! I have been and come back again."

The wolf felt very angry at this, so he said:

"Little pig, I know where there is a nice apple tree."

"Where?" said the pig.

"Down at Merry-garden," replied the wolf, "I will come for you at five o'clock tomorrow and get some apples."

Well, the little pig bustled up the next morning at four o'clock, and went off, hoping to get back before the wolf came; but he had further to go, and had to climb the tree, so that just as he was coming down from it, he saw the wolf coming which frightened him very much. The wolf came up and said:

"Little pig, are you here before me? Are they nice apples?"

"Yes, very," said the little pig. "I will throw you one."

And he threw it so far that while the wolf went to pick it up, the little pig jumped down and ran home.

The next day the wolf came again, and said:

"Little pig, there is a fair, will you go?"

"Oh yes," said the pig, "I will go; what time shall you be ready?"

"At three," said the wolf.

So the little pig went off before the time, and bought a butter-churn, which he was going home with when he saw the wolf coming. So he got into the churn to hide, but it rolled down the hill with the pig in it, which frightened the wolf so much that he ran home. He went to the little pig's house, and told him how frightened he had been. The little pig said:

"Hah, I frightened you, then. I went to the fair and bought a butter-churn. When I saw you, I got into it, and rolled down the hill."

Then the wolf was very angry, and declared he *would* eat up the little pig, and he would go down the chimney after him. When the little pig saw this, he hung a pot full of water on a blazing fire, and in fell the wolf; so the little pig put on the cover, boiled him up, and ate him for supper.

---

255   ALLEN, JONATHAN.   *Who's at the Door?.*

Tambourine Books, 1993

ISBN: 978-0-688-12257-7

Motifs: Animals (pigs)

               Animals (wolves or coyotes)

The three pigs live together in one house. The wolf wants to get in, but the pigs see through each of his disguises. Finally sick of his games, the pigs dress up as a wolf when he dresses as a pig, and they threaten to eat him if he doesn't leave them alone.

256   ASCH, FRANK.   *Ziggy Piggy and the Three Little Pigs.*

Kids Can Press, 1998

ISBN: 978-1-55074-515-3

Motifs: Animals (pigs)

               Animals (wolves or coyotes)

               Construction

Ziggy Piggy doesn't build a house of hay sticks or brick like his brothers, but chooses instead to sleep outdoors. When the wolf comes to town, his brothers hide inside their houses and Ziggy goes to the beach to swim and builds himself a raft with a sail. The two brothers are chased down to the beach and join Ziggy on the raft. When the wolf huffs and puffs and blows on the raft, all he does is blow the pigs out to sea and out of reach.

257   CELSI, TERESA NOEL.   *The Fourth Little Pig.*

Ill. by Doug Cushman. Raintree Publishers, 1990

ISBN: 978-0-8172-3577-2

Motifs: Animals (pigs)

               Animals (wolves or coyotes)

               Construction

Told in rhyming text. When the first three pigs hide from the wolf in the house of bricks, their sister, Pig Four, comes pounding on the door. She wants to know why they won't go outside and be active and shows them that there is actually nothing to be afraid of.

258   CHRISTELOW, EILEEN.   *Where's the Big Bad Wolf?.*
Clarion Books, 2002
ISBN: 978-0-618-18194-0
Motifs: Animals (pigs)
        Animals (wolves or coyotes)
        Construction

Narrated by Detective Doggedly, the faithful but bumbling local police dog. He is sure that Big Bad Wolf is up to something, but can't quite figure out what. In the meantime, the three pigs are getting building advice from a new "sheep" in town named Esmerelda.

259   COLLINS, SHEILA HÉBERT.   *Les Trois Cochons.*
Ill. by Patrick Soper. Pelican, 1999
ISBN: 978-1-56554-325-6
Country/Culture: Cajun
Motifs: Animals (pigs)
        Animals (wolves or coyotes)
        Construction

The story is similar to the original, but with a Cajun setting. The pigs use sugarcane, rice stalk, and oyster shells for building materials. The third pig outwits the wolf several times. Finally he manages to get the wolf to come down the chimney, where he is boiled into grillades for the pigs. Includes definitions and pronunciation guide for French Cajun words on each page, and a recipe for grillades and grits.

260   CRESP, GAEL.   *The Tale of Gilbert Alexander Pig.*
Ill. by David Cox. Barefoot Books, 1999
ISBN: 978-1-84148-215-6
Motifs: Music
        Animals (pigs)
        Animals (wolves or coyotes)

Gilbert Alexander the pig travels to a variety of different homes trying to elude the wolf. Each time Gilbert plays his trumpet, the wolf comes and threatens to eat the pig and steal the trumpet, and each time Gilbert escapes. Finally tired of being chased, Gilbert strikes a deal with the wolf where they become housemates, the wolf does the cooking, and Gilbert plays the trumpet for both to enjoy.

261   DAVIS, DONALD.   *The Pig Who Went Home on Sunday: An Appalachian Folktale.*

Ill. by Jennifer Mazzucco. August House Little Folk, 2004

ISBN: 978-0-87483-571-7

Country/Culture: Appalachia

Motifs: Animals (pigs)

Animals (foxes)

Construction

Each time Mama Pig sends one of her sons out to build his own house, the fox tricks the pig into building a house he can blow down. The third pig builds his house of stones like Mama said. He convinces the fox that hunters are out to get him, and comes home to Mama for Sunday dinner. Includes a note on the tale by the author.

262   GANTSCHEV, IVAN.   *The Three Little Rabbits: A Balkan Folktale.*

North-South Books, 2001

ISBN: 978-0-7358-1474-5

Country/Culture: Balkans

Motifs: Animals (rabbits or hares)

Animals (foxes)

Construction

The three little rabbits leave home to build their own burrows. Two don't dig into the ground like their mama told them to, but the last one does. Fox blows down the other houses, but when he sticks his head in the burrow, it gets stuck and he has to negotiate with the rabbit to get help.

263   GEIST, KEN.   *Three Little Fish and the Big Bad Shark.*

Ill. by Julia Gorton. Scholastic, 2007

ISBN: 978-0-439-71962-9

Motifs: Fish

Fish (sharks)

Oceans or sealife

Three fish go out to sea to build their own houses. Tim and Jim build theirs of seaweed and sand. Sister Kim builds hers deep in a sunken ship. The shark visits Tim and Jim and chews both houses up. The brothers move to their sister's house and when the shark tries to munch on that house, all his teeth fall out.

264 GORDON, DAVID. *The Three Little Rigs.*
Laura Geringer Books, 2005
ISBN: 978-0-06-058118-3
Motifs: Transportation (trucks)
Construction

Three trucks leave home to build their own garages. One builds his of wood, another of stone, and the last builds his of steel. One after another, the Big Bad Wrecking Ball tears them down until the little trucks get the big cranes to help them.

265 HARRIS, JIM. *The Three Little Dinosaurs.*
Pelican, 1999
ISBN: 978-1-56554-371-3
Motifs: Dinosaurs
Construction

The first two little dinosaurs build houses of grass and bricks, which T. Rex easily demolishes. The third dino builds his out of boulders, which T. Rex has to figure out how to destroy. Rex's brain is so small that he takes years to figure it out, and when he returns, the three little dinos have turned into great big dinos who chase Rex off.

266 HOOKS, WILLIAM H. *The Three Little Pigs and the Fox.*
Ill. by S. D. Schindler. Macmillan, 1989
ISBN: 978-0-02-744431-5
Motifs: Animals (pigs)
Animals (foxes)
Construction

As each gets too big for her house, Mama Pig sends her piglets out to build their own. The first two pigs are caught by the fox and hidden in his den. The third pig tricks the fox into jumping into a churn, which she seals and sends down the stream. She releases her two brothers and they all go to Mama's house for Sunday dinner.

267 KELLOGG, STEVEN. *The Three Little Pigs.*
HarperTrophy, 1997
ISBN: 978-0-688-08731-9
Motifs: Animals (pigs)
Animals (wolves or coyotes)
Food (breads or grains)

Mama pig turns her waffle-making business over to her three piglets so that she can retire. When the wolf starts causing problems, she comes out of retirement to help. After several tries at eating the piglets, the wolf gets baked in a waffle and sent into retirement.

268 LAIRD, DONIVEE MARTIN. *The Three Little Hawaiian Pigs and the Magic Shark.*
Ill. by Carol Jossem. Barnaby Books, 1981
ISBN: 978-0-940350-01-4
Country/Culture: Hawaii
Motifs: Animals (pigs)
      Fish (sharks)
      Construction

Three pigs leave home and build houses of pili grass, driftwood, and lava rock. A magic shark disguises himself as a shaved ice vendor and blows down the first pig's house. Then he dresses as a beach boy and blows in the second pig's house. At the third house he huffs and puffs so hard that he completely deflates himself like a balloon and the three pigs roll him up and throw him out with the garbage. Includes a glossary of Hawaiian words used and pronunciation guide.

269 LISH, TED. *The Three Little Puppies and the Big Bad Flea.*
Ill. by Charles Jordan. Munchweiler Press, 2001
ISBN: 978-0-7940-0000-4
Motifs: Animals (dogs)
      Clothing (shoes or boots)
      Construction

The three puppies build their houses out of things they like the best — duck feathers, dried leaves, and old shoes. The Big Bad Flea sneaks in through the keyhole, chases out the puppies, and decides to stay in the house made of shoes.

270 LOWELL, SUSAN. *The Three Little Javelinas.*
Ill. by Jim Harris. Northland Pub., 1992
ISBN: 978-0-87358-542-2
Country/Culture: Western
Motifs: Animals (pigs)
      Animals (wolves or coyotes)
      Construction

The three javelinas build their houses of tumbleweed, sticks, and adobe. The coyote who blows them down wants to eat the wild pigs with red hot chili sauce, but instead ends up as a coyote-shaped puff of smoke coming out of their stovepipe. Includes terms in English, Spanish, and Native

American Desert People (Tohono O'odham) and an author's note on the setting.

271   MARSHALL, JAMES.   *The Three Little Pigs.*
Dial Books for Young Readers, 1989
ISBN: 978-0-8037-0594-4
Motifs: Animals (pigs)
　　　　　Animals (wolves or coyotes)
　　　　　Cooking
　　　　　Construction

This stays close to the original, but the wolf eats the first two pigs. When the wolf gets to the third pig, the pig makes and breaks several promises to come out of his house. The wolf finally gets so aggravated that he jumps down the chimney and the pig cooks him for supper.

272   OSMOND, ALAN.   *Huff 'n' Puff.*
Ill. by Mace Warner. Ideals Children's Books, 1999
ISBN: 978-1-57102-147-2
Motifs: Animals (pigs)
　　　　　Animals (wolves or coyotes)
　　　　　Gender role reversal
　　　　　Construction

Two sons and the daughter of Hank, the brick-building pig, have to protect themselves from the Big Bad Wolf and his son, Fang. Two of the pigs still live in the brick house, one has built a house of steel, and the girl, Sally, was smart enough to build her house out of an armored vehicle and blow the wolves out of the house.

273   RUBIN, VICKY.   *The Three Swingin' Pigs.*
Ill. by Rhode Montijo. Henry Holt, 2007
ISBN: 978-0-8050-7335-5
Motifs: Animals (pigs)
　　　　　Animals (wolves or coyotes)
　　　　　Music (jazz)

The Three Pigs are a jazz music group that plays all over town. Big Bad Wolf is determined to catch up with and eat them, but when he finds them, the pigs teach him to blow the sax instead of houses and invite him to join the band. The trio becomes a quartet.

274   SALINAS, BOBBI.   *The Three Pigs: Nacho, Tito, and Miguel.*

Pinata Publications, 1998
ISBN: 978-0-934925-05-1
Country/Culture: Hispanic
Motifs: Animals (pigs)
Animals (wolves or coyotes)
Construction

Nacho, Tito, and Miguel build their homes out of straw, wood, and adobe. José the wolf blows the first two down and captures Nacho and Tito, but Miguel sends José on a series of errands meant to aggravate him. Finally, José ends up in a pot of hot green chile stew and Miguel rescues Nacho and Tito from the wolf's house. Bilingual, with a glossary of Spanish words and phrases, costume ideas, and a recipe for green chile stew.

275   SCIESZKA, JON.   *The True Story of the Three Little Pigs.*

Ill. by Lane Smith. Viking, 1989
ISBN: 978-0-670-82759-6
Motifs: Animals (pigs)
Animals (wolves or coyotes)
Cooking
Construction

This story is told from the wolf's point of view. Alexander T. Wolf insists that he is completely innocent and his actions misunderstood. He went to each pig's house looking to borrow a cup of sugar to make a cake. He happened to have a cold that made him sneezy, and that was how he accidentally blew the houses down.

276   TRIVIZAS, EUGENIOS.   *The Three Little Wolves and the Big Bad Pig.*

Ill. by Helen Oxenbury. Margaret K. McElderry Books, 1993
ISBN: 978-0-689-50569-0
Motifs: Animals (wolves or coyotes)
Animals (pigs)
Construction
Flowers

The three little wolves build themselves a house of bricks, but the Big Bad Pig knocks it down with a sledgehammer. Then they build a house of concrete, which the pig tears down with a pneumatic drill. Next they build a fortified house, but that gets blown up with dynamite. Finally, the wolves build a house of flowers. When the pig tries to blow it down, the beautiful scent changes his demeanor.

277 WALTON, RICK. *Pig, Pigger, Piggest.*
Ill. by Jimmy Holder. Gibbs-Smith, 1997
ISBN: 978-0-87905-806-7
Motifs: Animals (pigs)
Construction

Each of the three pigs builds his castle of mud, and each is approached by a different witch (Witch, Witcher, and Witchest) who rains on the castles. The castles all turn into huge mud puddles, which isn't so bad if you're a pig. So the three pigs marry the three witches, and they all live "sloppily" ever after.

278 WHATLEY, BRUCE. *Wait! No Paint!*
HarperCollins, 2001
ISBN: 978-0-06-028270-7
Motifs: Animals (pigs)
Animals (wolves or coyotes)
Construction

As the three pigs are being pursued by the wolf, the illustrator of the book runs out of red paint and can't finish the pictures. He paints them a variety of wrong colors and patterns until they insist he change the storyline. So the illustrator paints the pigs in bear suits and changes the story to Goldilocks.

279 WIESNER, DAVID. *The Three Pigs.*
Clarion Books, 2001
ISBN: 978-0-618-00701-1
Motifs: Animals (pigs)
Animals (wolves or coyotes)
Dragons

When the wolf blows in the first pig's house, the pig gets blown off the picture panel. All the pigs soon discover that there is more to their reality than they first thought. They go visit other fairy tales to find the right type of beast to help them.

TORTOISE AND THE HARE

As published in *Æsop's Fables: A New Revised Version from Original Sources* . . . (Frank F. Lovell & Company, 1884).

A HARE ONE DAY RIDICULED THE SHORT FEET AND SLOW pace of the Tortoise. The latter, laughing, said: "Though you be swift as the wind, I will beat you in a race." The Hare, deeming her assertion to be simply impossible, assented to the proposal; and they agreed that the Fox should choose the course, and fix the goal. On the day appointed for the race they started together. The Tortoise never for a moment stopped, but went on with a slow but steady pace straight to the end of the course. The Hare, trusting to his native swiftness, cared little about the race, and lying down by the wayside, fell fast asleep. At last waking up, and moving as fast as he could, he saw the Tortoise had reached the goal, and was comfortably dozing after her fatigue.

Perseverance is surer than swiftness.

280 BERNSTEIN, DAN. *The Tortoise and Hare Race Again.*
Ill. by Andrew Glass. Holiday House, 2006
ISBN: 978-0-8234-1867-1
Motifs: Animals (rabbits or hares)
Animals (tortoises or turtles)

Hare can't stand all the criticism for losing the race, and Tortoise can't handle the celebrity. They agree to race again, both hoping the result will be right this time. But Hare still can't manage to stay awake the whole race. So Tortoise wears a rabbit disguise across the finish line to set everything right again.

281　BRUCHAC, JOSEPH, AND JAMES BRUCHAC.　*Turtle's Race with Beaver: A Traditional Seneca Story.*

Ill. by Jose Aruego and Ariane Dewey. Dial Books for Young Readers, 2003
ISBN: 978-0-8037-2852-3
Country/Culture: Native American (Seneca)
Motifs:　Animals (beavers)
　　　　　Animals (tortoises or turtles)

Beaver builds a dam in Turtle's pond and doesn't want to share the water. The two agree to race in order to decide who gets to live in the pond. Turtle wins the race by holding on to Beaver's tail, biting him at the last minute, and getting thrown over the finish line.

282　CORWIN, OLIVER J.　*Hare and Tortoise Race to the Moon.*

Harry N. Abrams, 2002
ISBN: 978-0-8109-0566-5
Motifs:　Animals (rabbits or hares)
　　　　　Animals (tortoises or turtles)
　　　　　Space

An updated version of the race tale, with the animals racing off in spaceships that they made themselves. Although Tortoise doesn't have a superfast ship like Hare, he gets to the moon first. When they both get to the finish line, they remain best friends and play together in space.

283　CUYLER, MARGERY.　*Road Signs: A Harey Race with a Tortoise.*

Ill. by Steve Haskamp. Winslow Press, 2000
ISBN: 978-1-890817-23-7
Motifs:　Animals (rabbits or hares)
　　　　　Animals (tortoises or turtles)

A standard updated version of the tale. The text is completely limited to road signs and placards held by the animal spectators along the race route. Instead of falling asleep, Hare makes several stops along the way, including the rest room, getting ice cream, and driving a circus train.

284   GRANOWSKY, ALVIN.   *Friends at the End.*

Steck-Vaughn, 1996

ISBN: 978-0-8114-7130-5

Motifs: Animals (rabbits or hares)

Animals (tortoises or turtles)

Part of the publisher's Point of View series. This edition tells the original tale in the first part, and then the book is turned over to read the hare's story. In the version narrated by the hare, he confesses that he learned a valuable lesson by losing the race to the tortoise. He found out that he didn't always have to win to be popular, and made more friends by admitting defeat.

285   LOWELL, SUSAN.   *The Tortoise and the Jackrabbit.*

Ill. by Jim Harris. Northland Pub., 1994

ISBN: 978-0-87358-586-6

Country/Culture: Western

Motifs: Animals (rabbits or hares)

Animals (tortoises or turtles)

This version is set in the Southwest and populated with desert animals. Roadrunner marks the race course, Rattlesnake marks the starting line, Buzzard judges from above, and Javelina, Gila Monster, Skink, and Deer watch from the sidelines. While Jackrabbit naps under a mesquite tree, Tortoise slowly makes her way across the desert and to the finish line. Includes an author's note on the setting.

286   MORA, PAT.   *The Race of Toad and Deer.*

Ill. by Domi. Groundwood Books, 2001

ISBN: 978-0-88899-434-9

Country/Culture: Hispanic

Motifs: Animals (frogs or toads)

Animals (deer)

Toad and Deer disagree on who is the fastest in the jungle, so they agree to race. Toad's friends position themselves along the race route and make sounds as if Toad is ahead of Deer. Deer runs so fast trying to catch up with the voice of Toad that he exhausts himself and loses the race.

287   REPCHUK, CAROLINE.   *The Race.*

Ill. by Allison Jay. Chronicle Books, 2002

ISBN: 978-0-8118-3500-8

Motifs: Animals (rabbits or hares)

Animals (tortoises or turtles)

The two friends set off on a race around the world. While Rabbit wastes time taking a variety of exotic transportation, Tortoise boards a steamship and has a quiet, uneventful trip to the finish line.

288   SYKES, JULIE.   *That's Not Fair, Hare!*
Ill. by Tim Warnes. Barron's Educational Series, 2001
ISBN: 978-0-7641-5347-1
Motifs: Animals (rabbits or hares)
    Animals (tortoises or turtles)

Hare is very greedy and wants all the cabbages for himself. When the two race to the cabbage field, Hare taunts Tortoise for being slow, but Tortoise stops several times to help friends along the way. When they get to the field, Tortoise challenges Hare to one more race that he knows he can win — getting home.

289   VOZAR, DAVID.   *M.C. Turtle and the Hip Hop Hare: A Nursery Rap.*
Ill. by Betsy Lewin. Doubleday Books for Young Readers, 1995
ISBN: 978-0-385-32157-0
Motifs: Animals (rabbits or hares)
    Animals (tortoises or turtles)
    Music (rap or hip-hop)

The story is set in an urban environment, and the text has a hip-hop beat. This time, the rabbit is delayed by attractions along the way, such as admiring chicken fans and a dance band. When the tortoise gets close to the finish line, he trips and rolls down a hill the rest of the way, narrowly beating the swaggering rabbit.

THE TURNIP

The version of "The Turnip" described in *Russian Fairy Tales Collected by Aleksandr Afanas'ev* is the briefest account. Less than 300 words, it relates the efforts of farm residents to extract a giant turnip from the ground. There is no introduction, descriptive text, or conclusion. The implied moral is that more can be accomplished when people work together than alone, but narrative is absent. Amusement is found in its telling and the cumulative or repetitive style in which each of the helpers' effort is repeated each time another is added. Afanas'ev's version begins with a grandfather who plants a turnip. The turnip grows so large he cannot pull it out of the ground, so he calls grandmother to help. Grandmother pulls on grandfather, and grandfather pulls on the turnip, but they still can't retrieve the turnip. Other participants in this account include a grandchild, a puppy, and five beetles, but other characters and produce can be used.

290 BERGER, THOMAS. *The Mouse and the Potato.*
Ill. by Carla Grillis. Floris Books, 1990
ISBN: 978-0-86315-103-3
Motifs: Fruits and vegetables (potatoes)
Animals (mice or rats)
Farms
A farmer finds a large potato growing in his field, and his daughter re-plants it. When it is time to harvest it, it takes every person in the family and every animal on the farm down to the littlest mouse to help to pull it out of the ground.

291　DAVIS, AUBREY. *The Enormous Potato.*
Ill. by Dusan Petricic. Kids Can Press, 1998
ISBN: 978-1-55074-386-9
Motifs: Fruits and vegetables (potatoes)

A farmer plants the eye of a potato and it grows and grows until it is the biggest potato in the world. To harvest it he must get help. He first enlists his wife, then his daughter, then the dog and the cat, but they can't get it out. When the mouse comes to help they finally manage to get it out of the ground.

292　HESTER, DENIA LEWIS. *Grandma Lena's Big Ol' Turnip.*
Ill. by Jackie Urbanovic. Albert Whitman, 2005
ISBN: 978-0-8075-3027-6
Motifs: Fruits and vegetables (turnips)

One of the turnips Grandma Lena planted is much bigger than the others. Try as she might, she cannot get the vegetable out of the ground. Friends, family, and neighbors all try to pull it out, but it's not until Baby Pearl helps that they can all enjoy it.

293　SILVERMAN, ERICA. *The Big Pumpkin.*
Ill. by S. D. Schindler. Simon & Schuster, 1992
ISBN: 978-0-02-782683-8
Motifs: Holidays (Halloween)
　　　　　Monsters, beasts, or magical creatures
　　　　　Fruits and vegetables (pumpkins)

Witch plants a pumpkin to make a pie, but it grows so large she needs help getting it out of the garden. Mummy, Vampire, Ghost, and Bat each try to help her get it out of the ground, but it isn't until they all pull together that they are successful and Witch can make her pie.

294　VAGIN, VLADIMIR. *The Enormous Carrot.*
Scholastic, 1998
ISBN: 978-0-590-45491-9
Motifs: Fruits and vegetables (carrots)
　　　　　Animals (rabbits or hares)
　　　　　Farms

Daisy and Floyd Rabbit plant a garden and one of the carrots grows so large that they can't get it out of the ground. All the animals on the farm try to help Daisy and Floyd, but it is not until the smallest mouse comes to help that the vegetable is harvested.

THE TWELVE DANCING PRINCESSES

Abridged from "The Shoes That Were Danced to Pieces" in *Household Tales by Brothers Grimm,* translated by Margaret Hunt (G. Bell and Sons, 1884).

THERE WAS A KING WHO HAD TWELVE DAUGHTERS. They slept in one room with their beds side by side, and at night the King bolted the door. But every morning, the daughters' shoes were worn out from dancing. So the King announced that whoever found where they danced should have one for his wife, but that whoever tried and failed would be killed. It was not long before a King's son offered to undertake the enterprise. Many tried, but all gave their lives for the effort.

One day a soldier found himself in the town where the King lived. There an old woman asked him where he was going.

"I don't know," he answered. "Maybe I will find where the princesses dance and marry one."

"You can," said the old woman, "if you do not drink the wine that they serve you. Pretend to be sound asleep, and use this cloak. It will make you invisible so you can follow them."

So the soldier went to the King and announced himself. That evening he was shown to the ante-chamber, and the eldest daughter brought him a glass of wine, which he pretended to drink. Then he lay down and began to snore loudly. When the twelve heard this they got up, dressed themselves, thrilled to go to the dance.

Only the youngest said, "Something is odd, some misfortune is about to befall us."

"That's silly," said the eldest. "How many have already tried to find out our se-cret? I gave the soldier a sleeping-draught just like the others. He will not awaken."

When they were ready, they checked the soldier once more, but he still slept soundly. Then they each descended through a door hidden under one bed. The sol-dier, who had watched everything through half-closed eyes, put on his cloak and followed them. Halfway down the steps, he trod on the dress of the youngest. She was startled and cried out.

"Who is pulling my dress?"

"Don't be silly!" said the eldest. "You have caught it on a nail."

When the princesses were at the bottom of the steps, they stood in an avenue of trees with leaves of silver. The soldier broke off a twig from one of them in order to show the King on his return, but the tree cracked with a loud report.

The youngest girl cried out, "Something is wrong, did you hear the crack?"

But the eldest said, "It is only a gun fired for joy, because we have returned."

Then they came to an avenue where all the leaves were of gold, and lastly into a third where they were of bright diamonds. The soldier broke off a twig from each of these and each time it made such a noise that the youngest jumped in fright. Still the eldest maintained that these were salutes.

Finally the princesses came to a great lake where there were twelve little boats, and in every boat sat a handsome prince waiting for the twelve. The soldier seated himself in the boat with the youngest. Her prince said, "Why is the boat heavy? It takes all my strength to row."

Opposite the lake stood a splendid castle, and music resounded from within. The twelve entered, and each prince danced with the girl he loved. There they danced until all the shoes were worn out, and they were forced to leave. They left their princes on the shore and promised to return the next night. When they reached the stairs the soldier ran and lay down in his bed, and when the twelve passed him they laughed at his fate.

The next morning the soldier said nothing, but waited to watch again. That evening everything was the same, and the third night too. When the time came for the soldier to meet the King, the twelve stood behind the door, and listened.

"Where do my twelve daughters dance their shoes to pieces each night?" the King asked.

"In an underground castle with twelve princes," answered the soldier, and he told about the dancing and presented the king with the tokens.

The King called his daughters, and asked if this was the truth. The princesses saw that they were caught, and confessed. The King asked the soldier which of the girls he wanted for a wife.

He answered, "I am no longer young, so give me the eldest."

The wedding was celebrated that day, and the kingdom was promised to the soldier after the King's death. And the secret princes were bewitched for each night they had danced with the twelve.

295   ALLEN, DEBBIE.   *Brothers of the Knight.*

Ill. by Kadir Nelson. Dial Books for Young Readers, 1999
ISBN: 978-0-8037-2488-4
Country/Culture: African American
Motifs: Dancing
Music (big band)
Gender role reversal

Set in "a little village named Harlem." The protagonists are twelve sons of
the good Reverend Knight. With the help of a small kitchen elf, they go
out dancing at the Big Band Ballroom every night, but are discovered by
the nanny, Sunday, who knows a few slick steps of her own.

296   BATEMAN, TERESA.   *The Princesses Have a Ball.*

Ill. by Lynne Woodcock Cravath. Albert Whitman, 2002
ISBN: 978-0-8075-6626-8
Motifs: Clothing (shoes or boots)
Sports (basketball)

These princesses are all too tall to dance well, but every morning they
come to breakfast exhausted, disheveled, and with holes in their shoes.
The clever cobbler who is charged with repairing the shoes finds out that
the ball the princesses attend every night is a basketball league.

297   FITCHETT, GORDON.   *The Twelve Princesses.*

Phyllis Fogelman Books, 2000
ISBN: 978-0-8037-2474-7
Motifs: Birds (ducks)
Clothing (shoes or boots)

An account of the original story, with the main characters portrayed as
ducks. Several duck princes try to find out how the princesses wear out
their shoes every night, but all fail until one duck meets an old woman in
the forest. She tells him to try to find the secret, but warns him not to
drink the wine the princesses offer him, and gives him a cloak of invisi-
bility so he can follow them and not be seen.

298   PANCHERI, JAN.   *The Twelve Poodle Princesses.*
Red Fox, 1996
ISBN: 978-0-09-933721-8
Motifs: Animals (dogs)
        Dancing

A rewrite of the original tale, but with the main characters as dogs. The mongrel Valentine is the dog who finds out the princesses' secret, but the poodle princesses are such malcontents that he chooses not to marry any of them and returns home with the money to marry his sweetheart, Polly.

THE UGLY DUCKLING

Abbreviated from: Andersen, Hans. *The Complete Andersen: All of the 168 Stories by Hans Christian Andersen (Some Never Before Translated into English, and a Few Never Before Published) Now Freshly Translated [. . .] by Jean Hersholt* (The Limited Editions Club, 1949).

THERE ONCE WAS A MOTHER DUCK WHO SPENT MANY DAYS sitting on her eggs, waiting for them to hatch. It was boring, and she wished they would hurry. Finally, on a beautiful spring day, she heard the pecks she had been waiting for. Throughout the morning, they pecked and pecked until, One! Two! Three! Out popped her ducklings from their eggshells. They were beautiful, and the mother duck was so proud of them. But one egg, the largest egg in the nest, did not hatch. "Well," thought the mother duck, "the others are so beautiful, it seems a shame to give up now." So she continued to sit on the huge egg, hoping it would hatch soon.

Finally, the egg began to hatch. After several hours, her last duckling emerged. But my! He didn't look like the others at all! While her other ducklings were yellow and fluffy and perfect, this one was big and gangly and grey. "Humph!" The mother duck sighed, "I certainly hope he can swim!"

So she took all the ducklings down to the pond, but that's when things got worse. The other duck families were not happy to share the water with yet another brood, especially one that had such an offensive-looking member. "What on earth happened to him?" asked an old drake. "I believe he stayed in the egg too long," replied the mother. "It's such a pity, too. The others are so beautiful!"

Soon the whole pond was agog with the news of the very ugly duckling. Embarrassed, his siblings tried to chase him away, but when they did, other ducklings would start pecking at him. Finally, after several days of this, the ugly duckling decided there was nothing left for him to do but run away. And run he did, because he couldn't yet fly. When he could run no longer, he stopped at a marsh. "This looks like a comfortable place," he thought to himself. He swam about a bit, drinking the water and snapping at bugs and such. Then suddenly, Blam! Blam! Blam! Three bullets whizzed by his head, splashing into the water around him. "Ahhhh!" he screamed and dove for the reeds. "I guess this isn't such a safe place after all." He waited a bit for everything to settle down, and then he started off again.

The little duckling wandered for months. He would stop here and there along his way to find food or shelter, but every time he would settle into a place, the other animals would chase him or peck at him until he moved along. The winter was especially bad. He was so cold and lonely, and all he wanted was a place where he could feel comfortable and have friends who loved him as he was.

One day, when the weather seemed to be warming a bit, the ugly duckling found himself, weary and hungry, at yet another small pond. "I don't care any more," he thought, "Come what may, this is where I'm going to stay." And he wandered about looking for a place to take a nap. He spied a clump of reeds on the far side of the pond, and determined that was where he was going to sleep. As he got closer he heard a rustling coming from the marsh, and out swam several large, white, regal-looking birds. The ugly duckling had never seen such birds before, and he wanted so much to be like them that his heart ached. "Honk! Honk! Honk!" The big birds laid eyes on him. They got very excited and rushed forward. "I'm not leaving," he resolved. "They can kill me if they like, but I will not run away again!" And he bowed his head, waiting for the attack. But when he did this, an amazing thing occurred. He saw his reflection in the silvery water, and found that he was not the ugly duckling that he had been. In fact, now he looked just like those magnificent birds who were almost upon him! And then they were there, not pecking and harassing as he expected, but patting and preening and welcoming him as if he was a lost brother. "Why are you alone?" they cried. "What happened to your flock? You must come with us!" And they took him into the reeds with them, cleaned and fed him, and determined that he should be part of their family. And you know what? The beautiful swan did stay in that pond, and he lived happily ever after.

299   CRUMP, FRED H.   *The Ebony Duckling.*
Winston-Derek Publishers, 1992
ISBN: 978-1-55523-457-7
Country/Culture: African American
Motifs: Birds (ducks)
Birds (swans)

An ebony duckling is hatched into a family of beautiful ducks. He leaves in search of a new family where he can feel loved and wanted. He searches and searches, but no one will offer him a home. Convinced that he will never find a place to belong, this ugly duckling discovers how precious and rare he really is. He turns into an ebony swan, the most beautiful bird on the farm.

300   GORDON, DAVID. *The Ugly Truckling.*
Laura Geringer Books, 2004
ISBN: 978-0-06-054600-7
Motifs: Transportation (trucks)
Transportation (airplanes)

The little truck can't figure out why he doesn't look and act like his brothers and sisters. One day he looks at his reflection in a pond and sees something flying overhead and realizes that he is an airplane instead of a truck.

The Wolf and the Seven Little Kids

Abridged from *Household Stories by the Brothers Grimm* (Macmillan and Company, 1886).

There was once an old goat who had seven little ones. One day she had to go into the wood to fetch food for them, so she called them all round her.

"Dear children," said she, "I am going out into the wood; and while I am gone, be on your guard against the wolf, for he will eat you up. The wretch often disguises himself, but he may always be known by his hoarse voice and black paws."

"Dear mother," answered the kids, "you need not be afraid, we will take good care of ourselves." And the mother bleated good-bye, and went on her way.

It was not long before someone came knocking at the house-door, crying out,

"Open the door, my dear children, your mother is back." But the little kids knew it was the wolf by the hoarse voice.

"We will not open the door," cried they; "Our mother has a delicate and sweet voice, and your voice is hoarse; you must be the wolf."

Then off went the wolf to a shop and bought a big lump of chalk, and ate it up to make his voice soft. And then he came back, knocked on the door, and cried,

"Open the door, my dear children, your mother is here."

But the wolf had put up his black paws against the window, and the kids seeing this, cried out,

"We will not open the door; our mother has no black paws like you; you must be the wolf."

The wolf then ran to a baker.

"Baker," said he, "I am hurt in the foot; pray spread some dough over the place."

And when the baker had plastered his feet, he ran back to the house.

And now came the rogue the third time to the door and knocked. "Open, children!" cried he. "Your dear mother has come home, and brought you each something from the wood."

"First show us your paws," said the kids, "so that we may know if you are really our mother or not."

And he put up his paws against the window, and when they saw that they were white, all seemed right, and they opened the door; and when he was inside they saw it was the wolf, and they were terrified and tried to hide themselves. But the wolf found them all, and gave them short shrift; one after the other he swallowed down, all but the youngest, who was hid in the clock-case. And so the wolf strolled forth into the green meadows and fell asleep.

Not long after, the mother goat came back from the wood; and, oh! what a sight met her eyes! The door was standing wide open, table, chairs, and stools, all thrown about, dishes broken, quilt and pillows torn off the bed. She sought her children, they were nowhere to be found until she came to the name of the youngest in the clock-case.

And so she helped him out, and heard how the wolf had come, and eaten all the rest. In her grief she wandered out of doors, the youngest kid with her; and when they came into the meadow, they saw the wolf lying under a tree, snoring so that the branches shook. The mother goat looked at him carefully on all sides and noticed how something inside his body was moving and struggling.

"Dear me!" thought she, "can it be that my poor children are still alive?" And she sent the little kid back to the house for a pair of shears, and needle, and thread. Then she cut the wolf's body open, and no sooner had she made one snip than out came the head of one of the kids, and then another snip, and then one after the other the six little kids all jumped out alive and well.

"Now fetch some good hard stones," said the mother, "and we will fill his body with them, as he lies asleep."

And so they fetched some in all haste, and put them inside him, and the mother sewed him up so quickly again that he was none the wiser.

When the wolf at last awoke, and got up, the stones inside him made him feel very thirsty. So he went to a brook, and stooped to drink, but the heavy stones weighed him down and he fell over into the water and was drowned. And when the seven little kids saw it they came up running.

"The wolf is dead, the wolf is dead!" they cried, and taking hands, they danced with their mother all about the place.

301   CONOVER, CHRIS.   *Mother Goose and the Sly Fox.*
Farrar, Straus and Giroux, 1989
ISBN: 978-0-374-35072-7
Motifs: Birds (geese)
Animals (foxes)

This stays close to the original version, with the substitution of geese for goats and the addition of a lazy mouse who was supposed to be keeping his eye on the goslings while Mother Goose does her errands. When the fox sinks to the bottom of the river, he is nibbled on by fish and he runs terrified into the forest, never to be seen again.

302   KIMMEL, ERIC A.   *Nanny Goat and the Seven Little Kids.*
Ill. by Janet Stevens. Holiday House, 1990
ISBN: 978-0-8234-0789-7
Motifs: Animals (goats)
Animals (wolves or coyotes)

Mother Goat leaves her kids in the house while she goes out. The wolf pretends that he is the mother so they will let him in. When he finally gets in he eats them all, including Mother when she returns. But Mother has a pair of scissors in her apron that she uses to cut them all out of the wolf's stomach. They refill him with stones, and when the wolf goes to get a drink of water he falls into the river.

BIBLIOGRAPHY

Aarne, Antti, and Stith Thompson. *The Types of the Folktale: A Classification and Bibliography*. Second revision. Academia Scientarum Fennica, 1961.

Aesop. *Æsop's Fables: A New Revised Version from Original Sources with Upwards of 200 Illustrations by Harrison Weir, John Tenniel, Ernest Griset and Others*. Frank F. Lovell & Company, 1884.

Afanas'ev, Aleksandr. *Russian Folktales Collected by Aleksandr Afanas'ev*. Ill. by Alexander Alexeieff. Translated by Norbert Guterman. Pantheon, 1945.

Andersen, Hans. *The Complete Andersen, All of the 168 stories by Hans Christian Andersen (Some Never Before Translated into English, and a Few Never Before Published) Now Freshly Translated [. . .] by Jean Hersholt*. The Limited Editions Club, 1949.

Andersen, Hans. *Stories from Hans Andersen*. Ill. by Edmund Dulac. Hodder & Stoughton, 1911.

Asbjørnsen, Peter Christian, and Jørgen Moe. *Popular Tales from the Norse*. Translated by George Webbe Dasent. Third edition. David Douglas, 1888.

Ashliman, D. L. *Folk and Fairy Tales: A Handbook*. Greenwood Press, 2004.

Bettelheim, Bruno. *The Uses of Enchantment: The Meaning and Importance of Fairy Tales*. Alfred A. Knopf, 1976.

Booss, Claire (ed.). *Scandinavian Folk and Fairy Tales: Tales from Norway, Sweden, Denmark, Finland, Iceland*. Avenel Books, 1984.

Bryant, Sara Cone. *Stories to Tell Children: Fifty-Four Stories with Some Suggestions for Telling*. George G. Harrap & Co., 1918.

Dasent, George. *East o' the Sun and West o' the Moon: 59 Norwegian Folktales by George Webbe Dasent*. Dover, 1970.

Grimm, Jacob, and Wilhelm Grimm. *Household Stories by the Brothers Grimm.* Macmillan and Company, 1886.

_____. *Household Tales by Brothers Grimm.* Translated by Margaret Hunt. G. Bell and Sons, 1884.

Jacobs, Joseph. *English Fairy Tales.* Ill. by John Batten. Alfred A. Knopf, 1993.

_____. *English Fairy Tales Collected by Joseph Jacobs.* Third edition, revised. G.P. Putnam's Sons, 1902.

_____. *Europa's Fairy Book, Restored and Retold by Joseph Jacobs.* Ill. by John D. Batten. G.P. Putnam's Sons, 1916.

_____. *More English Fairy Tales Collected by Joseph Jacobs.* G.P. Putnam's Sons, n.d. [fourteenth impression].

Owens, Lily (ed.). *The Complete Brothers Grimm Fairy Tales.* Gramercy Books, 1981.

_____. *The Complete Hans Christian Andersen Fairy Tales.* Chatham River Press, 1981.

Perrault, Charles. *The Tales of Mother Goose as First Collected by Charles Perrault in 1696.* D.C. Heath & Co., 1901.

Tatar, Maria (ed.). *The Classic Fairy Tales.* W.W. Norton & Co., 1999.

Thompson, Stith. *The Folktale.* Holt, Rinehart and Winston, 1945.

_____. *Motif-Index of Folk-Literature; A Classification of Narrative Elements in Folktales, Ballads, Myths, Fables, Mediaeval Romances, Exempla, Fabliaux, Jest-Books, and Local Legends.* Revised and enlarged edition. Indiana University Press, 1955–1958.

Zipes, Jack (ed.). *Aesop's Fables.* Penguin, 1992.

_____. *The Oxford Companion to Fairy Tales: The Western Fairy Tale Tradition from Medieval to Modern.* Oxford University Press, 2000.

AUTHOR INDEX

References are to entry numbers, not page numbers.

TITLE INDEX

References are to entry numbers, not page numbers.

ILLUSTRATOR INDEX

References are to entry numbers, not page numbers. Where the author is also the illustrator, the name is not repeated as illustrator in the entry.

COUNTRY/CULTURE INDEX

References are to entry numbers, not page numbers.

MOTIF INDEX

References are to entry numbers, not page numbers.

B

C

S

SCHOOL

SEASONS (AUTUMN)

SEASONS (SPRING)

SEASONS (WINTER)

SPACE

SPORTS (BASKETBALL)

SPORTS (FOOTBALL)

SPORTS (SNOWBOARDING)

SPORTS (SURFING)

SPORTS (TRACK AND FIELD)

SPORTS (WRESTLING)

STARS

T

TEETH

TRANSPORTATION (AIRPLANES)

TRANSPORTATION (BOATS OR SHIPS)

TRANSPORTATION (BUSES)

TRANSPORTATION (CARS)

TRANSPORTATION (TRUCKS)

ABOUT THE AUTHORS

CATHARINE BOMHOLD is assistant professor of library and information science and director of the Fay B. Kaigler Children's Book Festival at the University of Southern Mississippi.

TERRI E. ELDER is a school media specialist with the Birmingham (AL) Public School District.